bare•

Number 10   Spring 2022

Editors
Peter Enfantino
John Scoleri

Layout
John Scoleri

Writers
Matthew R. Bradley
J. Charles Burwell
Gilbert Colon
Peter Enfantino
Richard Krauss
William Schoell
David J. Schow
John Scoleri
Jay Shepard
S. Craig Zahler

Cover
Ralph McQuarrie

***bare*•bones thanks**
Paula Ford
Vonna Gissler
Chris Matheson
Kurt Volkan

This issue is dedicated to
James Bama
(1926 - 2022)
Mitchell Ryan
(1934 - 2022)
Alan Ladd, Jr.
(1937 - 2022)
Neal Adams
(1941 - 2022)

Table of Contents

bare•bones is published by
Cimarron Street Books - Santa Clara, CA
cimarronstreetbooks.com

© 2022 Peter Enfantino & John Scoleri

ISBN: 979-880980-943-6

Contact us: CimarronStreetBooks@gmail.com

Those of you who know me may find it hard to believe that this issue's cover feature on *Star Wars* Expanded Universe fiction was in fact Peter's idea. While we were talking about future topics to cover in *bare•bones* a few months back, he indicated that he would be interested in reading an article on the best of the *Star Wars* spin-off novels that had been published through the years. While I'm a big fan of the films themselves, I have never warmed up to the fictional works by others playing in George's sandbox. Fortunately, I knew just the person to turn to, and Jay Shepard joins the *bare•bones* bullpen with his historical look at the *Star Wars* Expanded Universe, alongside a list of highlights from the past 45 years. This provided me with the perfect opportunity to showcase one of my late friend Ralph McQuarrie's paintings on the cover. You may recognize it from the first *original Star Wars* novel from 1978, **Splinter of the Mind's Eye**. Rather than just reprint the published cover, I wanted to feature Ralph's preliminary illustration, which is slightly different than the final painting (which you'll find reproduced on page 30). It's been 10 years since we lost Ralph, and I'm glad to pay tribute to his legacy with this cover.

I'm also pleased to present an interview with writer Chris Matheson, whose memoir, **Conversations with the Father: A Memoir about Richard Matheson, My Dad and God** will be released this summer. The book is a must-read for die-hard Matheson fans and scholars alike — and I hope the same can be said of our enlightening conversation.

David J. Schow's R&D column never disappoints, and this issue's installment is no exception. We think you'll enjoy the tale of his encounter with the 8th Wonder of the World as much as we did.

You'll find all that and more in the pages ahead. So what are you waiting for? Finish up these editorials so you can get to the meat of this issue (or meat substitute, if that's how you roll).

We'll see you in three months with another fresh serving of *bare•bones* . . .

John Scoleri
Santa Clara, CA
May 2022

If you happen to follow John and I on Facebook, you're well aware that the two of us seldom agree on the merits of a new Hollywood film. I'll lay into him for his cut-and-pasted remark that "he enjoyed *it* for what it was," regardless of whether *it* was a piece of crap or not. He'll remind me that I hate anything that was made post-1979 (and he's not far from wrong). I'm not as easily swayed by entertainment, especially if I left the comfort of my home and paid good money to be entertained.

We did, however, put aside our differences for the first time in a month of Sundays to agree on Matt Reeves's **The Batman**. John enjoyed it for what it was (*Actually, I said it was the most satisfying Batman film I've ever seen — ye other ed.*), while I insisted it must have been made in 1977 and put on a shelf until just the right time. Yes, the film has its faults (the pace is a tad, shall we say "slow," at times, and the Emo atmosphere can be grating) but I found it to be a fascinating and bold experiment; a steampunk variation on a 1939 issue of *Detective Comics*. And, aside from Christopher Nolan's Dark Knight trilogy and Patty Jenkins' first **Wonder Woman**, it's the only DC movie to get it "right."

John and I did *not* agree on Guillermo del Toro's remake of **Nightmare Alley**. I found it empty, garish, and poorly-cast. My dissatisfaction with the film has nothing to do with noir snobbery or a sense that fucking with an established classic is a big no-no. Yep, I think the original film (sans that cop-out climax) is a gut-punch and so much more atmospheric than the 2021 version, but my primary problems with del Toro's version is that it fills in *too many* of the details and that Bradley Cooper is all wrong for the part of Stanton Carlisle. I couldn't help feeling that Cooper was winking at his audience and calming their fears; the guy who sings country western stuff in that *other* remake is right there under all that greasepaint and vintage clothing.

Which nicely segues into our content this issue. Despite my dislike of the new **Nightmare Alley**, I found J. Charles Burwell's comparison of the source novel and its two film adaptations to be fascinating reading. Obviously, Burwell is just as wrong about the del Toro indiscretion as John but don't let that stop you from diving into this dissection. If anything it will either remind you just how unsettling the novel and the '47 adaptation are or nudge you into giving them a try.

Peter Enfantino
Gilbert, AZ
May 2022

HENRY FARRELL
The Godfather of *Grande Dame Guignol*
by Matthew R. Bradley

Call it what you will — *Grande Dame Guignol*, psycho-biddy cinema, hagsploitation — it all started with **What Ever Happened to Baby Jane?** (1962), starring Bette Davis and Joan Crawford, who notoriously hated each other as much as their characters, Jane and Blanche Hudson. The films in this subgenre, some similarly titled, revitalized the careers of many an aging actress as the perpetrator or victim of dastardly doings, often unhinged, gaslit and/or haunted by dire deeds of decades past. But as with Alfred Hitchcock and Robert Bloch's **Psycho** (1959), producer/director Robert Aldrich would have had nothing without a 1960 novel by Henry Farrell (1920-2006), born as Charles Farrell Myers in Madera, California.

He had already established himself as a pulp fantasy writer under his real name, Charles F. Myers, with the Toffee stories, starting with "I'll Dream of You" in the January 1947 issue of *Fantastic Adventures*. Six more followed there through "The Shades of Toffee" (June 1950), and a further three in *Imagination Stories of Science and Fantasy*, ending with "The Laughter of Toffee" (October 1954). Concerning a "dream girl" periodically escaping from the protagonist's mind into the real world, they were an apparent homage to the ghostly couple in Thorne Smith's **Topper** (1926) and **Topper Takes a Trip** (1932), a relationship made most patent by the title of Myers's "Toffee Takes a Trip" (July 1947).

Myers took the Farrell byline with his first novel, **The Hostage** (1959), adapted by Robert Laning into an eponymous 1967 feature directed by Russell S. Doughten, Jr., with Harry Dean Stanton and John Carradine. Between **Baby Jane**'s appearance on page and screen, another Farrell novel, **Death on the Sixth Day** (1961), became the *Bus Stop* episode "Jaws of Darkness" (12/31/61), directed by Stuart Rosenberg and scripted by Alvin Sargent. He appears to have been trying to break into screenwriting at the same time; a story credit on Robert Florey's *Alfred Hitchcock Presents* episode "Where Beauty Lies" (6/26/62) seems to represent not a published story, but an original script, rewritten by James P. Cavanagh.

In Farrell's prologue, set in 1908, vaudeville star Baby Jane — "The Diminutive Dancing Duse from Duluth" — shocks fans outside the theater by lording it over her father, Ray, as the breadwinner while her mother holds infant Blanche. Fast-forward to 1959 as Pauline Bates, their widowed next-door neighbor on Hollywood's Hillside Terrace, and her friend Harriet Palmer recall the car crash that paralyzed Blanche more than 20 years ago, ending her film stardom, and a contractual clause mandating a role in each for Jane, said to have caused the accident. Also watching **Moonlight on Fifth Avenue** on TV are

3

the sisters, setting off another of jealous, hard-drinking caregiver Jane's periodic venomous "spells."

While Blanche weighs advising business manager Bert Hanley that she's reversed herself about selling off their "white, two-story Mediterranean absurdity," cleaning woman Edna Stitt confides that Jane has been opening and withholding the fan letters she still receives. "Your sister is not a well woman," she tells Blanche — who recalls producer Martin Stagg cautioning 30 years ago that Jane's acting out would harm her career, and to get rid of the clause — but Blanche demurs. Eavesdropping on Blanche's attempt to contact Bert, Jane intercepts his return call, saying that she has changed her mind, and serves a rotting bird to Blanche, who finds the extension off the hook when trying to call Dr. Warren Shelby.

Jane continues the culinary warfare, sprinkling fine, white sand over her dinner the next night, and Blanche is about to drop a note from her barred upstairs window, asking Mrs. Bates to call Shelby, but fearing the possibility of adverse publicity, she decides to await Edna. Preventing their speaking privately, Jane then drives off to place a want ad: "Exp. accompanist-arranger, male, to join est. star in acts for clubs, TV. Piano, violin, req." On returning, she finds that Blanche has pulled herself out of her wheelchair and downstairs; catching her summoning Shelby, Jane drags her back upstairs, locks her in her room, and calls the doctor back, explaining in Blanche's voice that it was just a "misunderstanding."

The ad is answered by Edwin Flagg, a portly failed musician whose despised but adoring single mother, Del, has become too arthritic to support them as a domestic,

and after their first meeting, he agrees to return and discuss Jane's "comeback" further, smelling money. Abruptly fired by Jane, a skeptical Edna returns while she cashes Bert's allowance check, finding Blanche's door locked and evidence that Jane has forged her signature. Waylaid by Mrs. Bates, who gives her a clipping about Blanche's regained popularity on TV, Jane confronts Edna; threatened with the police, Jane opens the room, where Edna is shocked to see Blanche bound and gagged, and kills her with a hammer, dumping her in a ravine.

In a drunken stupor, Jane fails to open the door for Edwin, to whom Del later relates how, forced to return home from a wild party, Jane ran down Blanche as she tried to open their front gates. Remorseful over Edna, Jane unties Blanche, caught throwing the note out the window, but before Mrs. Bates can examine it, Harriet interrupts with a newspaper report about Edna. Desperate for money, Flagg returns and is drinking with Jane when Blanche, having heard his voice, dumps her dinner tray to alert him; confronted with the horrifying sight of the emaciated prisoner, he flees the house, and as he sits on the protective barrier beside a dangerous curve Jane drives right at him, sending him over onto the bluff below.

Seen and accused by Mrs. Bates, Jane drives Blanche to the beach as news hits the papers that Flagg survived, Blanche is missing, and Jane "sought on suspicion of murder"; while moving Blanche's coupé, blocking their garage, a young couple spots the registration and calls the police. Blanche confesses to switching places when Jane passed out at the wheel that fateful night, so she was actually driving

4

the car when she missed Jane — who fell out of the way and ran off — and hit the gates, letting everyone believe it was her sister. Jane is interrupted by the arrival of the police as she calls them from a phone booth herself but, asked to lead them to Blanche and increasingly detached from reality, begins to dance . . .

Screenwriter Lukas Heller — whose collaborations with Aldrich included two of his best, *The Flight of the Phoenix* (1965) and *The Dirty Dozen* (1967) — moves the prologue to 1917, with Julie Allred and Gina Gillespie as Jane and Blanche, respectively, and Dave Willock and Ann[e] Barton as their parents. He gives the wife a name, Cora, and changes others: Edna to Elvira (Maidie Norman), Stagg to McDonald (Wesley Addy), and Del to Dehlia (Marjorie Bennett). Harriet is supplanted by the teenaged daughter of Mrs. Bates (Anna Lee), Liza (Davis's real-life daughter, B[arbara].D. Merrill), while Blanche's old movie, which they watch on television, is represented by Crawford's own *Sadie McKee* (1934).

Although omitting the automotive attack on Flagg and adding Jane's plaintive line, "You mean all this time we could have been friends?," the film is otherwise extremely faithful. In his first of three roles for Aldrich, Victor Buono is letter-perfect as Flagg, with Robert Cornthwaite, so memorable as Dr. Carrington in *The Thing from Another World* (1951), as Shelby, and Maxine Cooper, indelible as Velma in Aldrich's *Kiss Me Deadly* (1955), in the small role of the bank teller. In the beach scene, the police officers include James Seay, the kindly gerontologist from *Miracle on 34th Street* (1947); Aldrich's son, third assistant director, and future associate producer, William, is the lunch counter assistant.

For Jane's signature song, "I've Written a Letter to Daddy," lyricist Bob Merrill expands on Farrell's original: "Oh, the postman, he won't mind/Cause Mama says that heaven's near./Tho' you've left us both behind,/I am writing, Daddy, dear./I l-o-v-e you!" Norma Koch's costume design won an Academy Award; Davis, Buono, and the film's veteran cinematographer,

Ernest Haller — who won for *Gone with the Wind* (1939) — were also nominated. Legend has it that the envious Crawford not only conspired with powerful gossip columnist Hedda Hopper to deny Davis her record third Oscar, but also arranged to accept the award on behalf of winner Anne Bancroft for *The Miracle Worker* (1962).

Bette's cruelly aborted nod was earned, given her deglamorization and histrionics: pasty-faced, slovenly, shuffling in her slippers, flinging aside the phone taken from Blanche's room, applying gobs of lipstick and a beauty mark. Milking the "innocent" victim to the hilt, Joan says, "You wouldn't be able to do these awful things to me if I weren't still in this chair," and Bette replies, after a well-timed smile and eye-roll, "Butcha *are*, Blanche. Ya *are* in that chair." In a nicely cinematic moment, a starving Blanche — afraid even to uncover her "din-din" after being served her pet bird — finds a rat, and as Jane maniacally cackles in the hall, she spins futilely in her wheelchair in a Hitchcockian overhead shot.

Aldrich generates suspense with cross-cutting when other characters try to capitalize on Jane's absence, placing the phone in the foreground for emphasis as Blanche makes her way painfully downstairs in the background, clinging to the rail, before Jane returns and kicks the crap out of her. Also memorable are Blanche wolfing down chocolates in her room, and an appalled Flagg's priceless expressions as the self-delusional Jane recreates her act in a booze-wrecked voice. Alternately fragile and ferocious, she truly does seem dangerously unpredictable, but it's hard not to empathize when Blanche stabs the buzzer that summons her, drowning out Jane's clearly mouthed "bitch" after "You miserable . . . "

Authorship of **Baby Jane** alone might have enthroned Farrell as the wellspring of *Grande Dame Guignol*, but he then became an active participant, sharing script credit with Heller on Aldrich's *Hush . . . Hush, Sweet Charlotte* (1964). Based on Farrell's then-unpublished novella "What Ever Happened to Cousin Charlotte?," it was to have reunited Davis with Crawford, replaced by Olivia de Havilland during production due to "illness." Curiously, the inventory of Boston University's Henry Farrell Collection suggests that, although it is credited solely to Luther Davis, the screenplay for de Havilland's previous film, *Lady in a Cage* (1964) — also replacing Crawford — was based on an unpublished novel by Farrell.

"Usual suspects" included composer Frank DeVol and actors Buono, Addy, and (as a taxi driver) Willock; newbies Joseph Cotten — aptly seen in the seminal *Gaslight* (1944) — and Agnes Moorehead were veterans of Orson Welles's Mercury Theatre. Cinematographer Joseph F. Biroc, who shot more than a dozen Aldrich films in a career stretching back to *It's a Wonderful Life* (1946), garnered one of the film's seven Oscar nominations, as did Moorehead, Koch and, for both song (with lyricist Mack David) and score, DeVol. In the 1927 prologue, after Charlotte's father, Big Sam Hollis (Buono), convinces married John Mayhew (Bruce Dern) not to elope with her, somebody chops off John's head and hand.

Believing it was Sam, Charlotte (Davis) — widely presumed guilty herself — has stayed in their Louisiana mansion ever since to protect his secret, receiving poison-pen letters that she attributes to John's widow, Jewel (Mary Astor). With Hollis House to be demolished for a bridge, Charlotte seeks the help of cousin Miriam Deering (de Havilland), who was jilted by Dr. Drew Bayliss (Cotten) due to the family scandal, but soon after she arrives, Charlotte begins seeing the severed body parts and hearing the title song, written for her by John. Jewel castigates Miriam for tipping off Sam, and insurance investigator Harry Willis (Cecil Kellaway) arrives, posing as a reporter to learn why she never filed a claim.

Housekeeper Velma Cruther (Moorehead) believes Miriam is after Charlotte's money — correctly, since she and Bayliss are trying to drive Charlotte insane and get control of the estate. Velma finds the hallucinogen he's been giving Charlotte, and threatens exposure, but Miriam hits her with a chair, knocking her downstairs to her death; Charlotte shoots Drew, "seeing" the mutilated John, and dumps the body in the swamp with Miriam. In a nod to Henri-Georges Clouzot's *Les Diaboliques* (1955), he returns, covered with mud, and Charlotte's mind snaps . . . until she hears Miriam reveal that she wrote the letters and blackmailed Jewel, who really killed John, and pushes a huge stone bowl onto the lovers.

Like de Havilland, Davis and Astor were under contract in the 1930s to Warner Brothers, where they starred in the second and third versions of Dashiell Hammett's **The Maltese Falcon** (1927), respectively *Satan Met a Lady* (1936) and the 1941 John Huston classic. Speaking of coincidences, that same year, Dern played another victim whose murder will set things in motion decades later in Alfred Hitchcock's *Marnie* (1964). Bette was billed above Olivia in *It's Love I'm After* (1937), *The Private Lives of Elizabeth and Essex* (1939), and *In This Our Life* (1942), and above Astor in *The Great Lie* (1941), so their shared history again provides interesting context, although both were friends off-screen.

It's difficult to imagine that Crawford could have played Miriam as well as de Havilland, spitting venom at Charlotte ("You wretched idiot!") and slapping her around; the gleeful Moorehead voraciously devours any scenery left unchewed by Davis, and their Southern-fried vocalizations are troweled on as thickly as Jane's pancake. Interestingly, in a 1935 *Baby Jane* scene of director Ben Golden (Bert Freed) and Marty watching footage from *Parachute Jumper* (1933) — reportedly Davis's least favorite of her films — intended to demonstrate that "she stinks," he says, "She has a Southern accent like I have a Southern accent." Although she lived until 1987, Astor retired after playing the dying Jewel here.

Released through Fox rather than Warner's, *Charlotte* had a bigger budget than *Jane* and a strong supporting cast, e.g., Roger Corman regular William Campbell as sleazy *Crimes of Passion* photog Paul Marchand. It reunited veterans of *Kiss Me Deadly*, with Aldrich mainstay Addy — Mike Hammer's police pal, Pat — as sympathetic Sheriff Luke Standish and Percy Helton as the funeral director, and *It's a Wonderful Life*, with the sassy Annie, Lillian Randolph, and Ellen Corby ("Could I have $17.50?") as, respectively, a cleaning woman and a town gossip. Buono, then 26, convincingly looks 44; George Kennedy, the foreman, was beheaded à la Dern in William Castle's *Strait-Jacket* (1964) the same year.

After *Charlotte*, Farrell scripted two *Perry Mason* episodes, "The Case of the Wrathful Wraith" (11/7/65) and " . . . Bogus Buccaneers" (1/9/66), both directed by Arthur Marks. A change in gender would have placed *How Awful About Allan* (9/22/70) perfectly in the hagsploitation mold (it did co-star non-*ingénues* Julie Harris and Joan Hackett); Anthony Perkins plays a gaslit ex-mental patient recovering from psychosomatic blindness, while Farrell's wife, Molly Dodd, appears briefly as an unidentified patient. Directed by Curtis Harrington, it was adapted by Farrell from his 1963 novel, which German writer-director Peter Lilienthal had made into another telefilm, *Horror* (1/13/69), only the previous year.

Soon afterward, Farrell adapted *The House That Would Not Die* (10/27/70) from **Ammie, Come Home** (1968), the first in the Georgetown Trilogy by Barbara Michaels, followed by **Shattered Silk** (1986) and **Stitches in Time** (1995). Michaels was a pseudonym for the Egyptologist Barbara Mertz, who also wrote the Amelia Peabody mysteries as Elizabeth Peters. British director John Llewellyn Moxey had made his feature-film debut with *The City of the Dead* (aka *Horror Hotel*, 1960), a proto-Amicus production co-starring Christopher Lee; barely a year after *House*'s Halloween-timed airing, he launched Carl Kolchak's career, and set viewership records, with another ABC Movie of the Week, *The Night Stalker* (1/11/72).

Inheriting and occupying a colonial house with her niece, Sara Dunning (Kitty Winn), Ruth Bennett (Barbara Stanwyck) meets her new neighbor, anthropology professor Pat McDougal (Richard Egan), and his student Stan Whitman (Michael Anderson, Jr.). Billed in her screen debut here as Katherine, Winn would be better known as Chris MacNeil's secretary, Sharon Spencer, in *The Exorcist* (1973), and was killed off in *Exorcist II: The Heretic* (1977). Pat's Aunt Delia (Mabel Albertson) introduces Ruth to medium Sylvia Wall (Doreen Lang), who suggests a séance at the house; Sara buys a portrait of a Revolutionary officer that discomfits Pat, while Ruth dreams of her crying for help and hears a voice call, "Ammie, come home."

Pat violently kisses Ruth before the séance, during which a face appears over Sara's and the portrait — repaired after it was found damaged — flies into the fire; later that night she attacks Ruth, recalling nothing in the morning, which Pat attributes to schizophrenia. But when she denies being Sara in another voice, Stan suggests possession, and tells Ruth that Pat may be affected. In the attic they find a journal, saved by Stan when a wind from the cellar blows it into the fire, and a scroll showing that Ruth's ancestor, widower General Douglas Campbell, became a recluse after his daughter, Amanda, vanished, so they hold a second séance, where wind once again blows open the door to the cellar, part of which Stan discovers is sealed off.

Pat and Sara locate a newspaper ad in which Campbell begged Amanda, who had reputedly eloped with Captain Anthony Doyle, to return; as a possessed

Pat is about to kill Stan with a poker, Ruth knocks him out. Through Sara, Ammie reveals that after Doyle confronted him with the knowledge that he was a traitor who had plotted with the British, Campbell killed them, but the discovery of the truth and the bodies buried in the cellar lays their Earthbound spirits to rest. While transposing the setting from Georgetown to Gettysburg, Pennsylvania, Farrell for the most part condenses the Michaels novel faithfully and skillfully, although his most significant interpolation — the portrait, presumably of Doyle — is never fully explained.

This marked the TV-movie debut of Stanwyck, who'd had a more overtly hagsploitative role as a gaslit widow, opposite off-screen ex-husband Robert Taylor, in her final feature, the Castle/Bloch outing *The Night Walker* (1964). But Farrell's last true *Grande Dame Guignol* credit was the original script for Harrington's *What's the Matter with Helen?* (1971), starring Debbie Reynolds and Shelley Winters; Moorehead returned, with Dodd in another minor role as Mrs. Rigg. Lucien Ballard photographed numerous features and TV episodes for Sam Peckinpah, most notably *The Wild Bunch* (1969), while composer David Raksin's decades-long career included the haunting title song from *Laura* (1944).

The film opens with 1930s *Hearst Metrotone News* footage into which Harrington inserts an item about Leonard Hill and Wesley Bruckner being sentenced to life for the killing of Ellie Banner in Braddock, Iowa. As their respective mothers, Helen (Winters) and Adelle (Reynolds), leave the courthouse, Helen is cut by an unseen figure in the crowd who later threatens them with anonymous phone calls. So, changing their last names to Martin and Stuart, they move to Hollywood, where Adelle opens a dance school for wannabe Shirley Temples, with Helen banging out "Goody Goody" on the piano; one mother, Mrs. Barker, is portrayed by Yvette Vickers, fondly remembered in *Attack of the 50 Foot Woman* (1958).

Soon after Helen relates that 4-year-old

Lenny saw his father, Matt (Gary Combs), killed in a ploughing accident for which he blamed her, Hamilton Starr (Michael MacLiammóir) is hired to teach drama and elocution. Dennis Weaver — the star of another legendary ABC Movie of the Week, Steven Spielberg and Richard Matheson's *Duel* (1971) — plays wealthy Lincoln Palmer, father of Winona (Sammee Lee Jones), who squires Adelle to an offshore gambling ship, where he hires a gigolo (Swen Swenson) to sub for him in a tango. This and other numbers choreographed by Tony Charmoli, who was nominated for 15 Emmy Awards between 1955 and 1998 (winning three), permitted Reynolds to strut her terpsichorean stuff.

Their recital is disrupted as a backstage incident makes Helen — increasingly obsessed over blades and her family tragedies — scream, prompting her partner to pose the titular question (Winters was reportedly having her own mental issues at the time). The next day, they find a "bloody" standee of Adelle in her dance costume, hacked up with a knife, while someone anonymously mails Linc a clipping about the trial, so he offers to help with a new lawyer for an appeal. Helen sees a shadowy figure watching the house, believing he'd made the phone calls; refuses a letter addressed to her real name; and fixates on Sister Alma (Moorehead) of the Church of the Open Hand (a radio evangelist modeled on Aimee Semple McPherson).

When a Man (Allen Pinson) enters the house, calling her Mrs. Hill, a terrified Helen pushes him downstairs; Adelle finds a letter saying that he tried to inform her of an inheritance, and they dump him in a construction site, where he is thought to have fallen by accident. Adelle forestalls a confession to Sister Alma, then agrees to elope with Linc, but at the house, she is stabbed by Helen (toned down, as a lesbian kiss between them was cut, to prevent an R rating), who slaughtered her own pet rabbits. Detective Sgt. West (Logan Ramsey) reveals that said Man really *was* Banner's vengeful lover, and as Linc arrives to pick up Adelle, he finds her body propped up like the cutout, with

So you met someone and now you know how it feels. Goody, Goody.

MARTIN RANSOHOFF presents
DEBBIE REYNOLDS | SHELLEY WINTERS
"WHAT'S THE MATTER WITH HELEN?"

DENNIS WEAVER
MICHEAL MacLIAMMOIR and
AGNES MOOREHEAD
Executive Producer EDWARD S. FELDMAN
Written by HENRY FARRELL
Produced by GEORGE EDWARDS
Directed by CURTIS HARRINGTON
A FILMWAYS-RAYMAX Production
GP
COLOR by DeLuxe
United Artists

Helen manically playing "Goody Goody."

Veteran art director Eugène Lourié served as the production designer on *Burnt Offerings* (1976), co-starring Davis, while his briefer directorial career included no fewer than three dinosaur films: *The Beast from 20,000 Fathoms* (1953), *The Giant Behemoth* (1959), and *Gorgo* (1961). The legendary makeup artist, William Tuttle, worked on a dozen *Twilight Zone* episodes, and won an honorary Oscar for *7 Faces of Dr. Lao* (1964), one of his five collaborations with producer George Pal. The novelization — which, like the poster, gave away the ending *on the front cover* — was by Richard Deming, a frequent contributor to *Alfred Hitchcock's Mystery Magazine* and *Manhunt* who specialized in television tie-ins.

In 1972, Farrell had a story and a shared script credit (with Stanford Whitmore) on Reza Badiyi's telefilm *The Eyes of Charles Sand* (2/29/72), starring *Dark Shadows* matriarch Joan Bennett, and François Truffaut adapted his 1967 novel **Such a Gorgeous Kid Like Me** with Jean-Loup Dabadie as *Une Belle Fille comme Moi* (*A Gorgeous Girl Like Me*). His imprint on *Grande Dame Guignol* shows in films with but one degree of separation. Davis followed with **Dead Ringer** (1964) and,

for Hammer, *The Nanny* (1965) and *The Anniversary* (1968), as did Crawford with Castle's *Strait-Jacket*, also written by Bloch, and *I Saw What You Did* (1965), plus Herman Cohen's *Berserk* (1967) and *Trog* (1970).

Aldrich produced *What Ever Happened to Aunt Alice?* (1969), starring Geraldine Page and Ruth Gordon, and directed the somewhat hagsploitative *The Legend of Lylah Clare* (1968) and *The Killing of Sister George* (1968), showcasing Kim Novak and Beryl Reid, respectively. Joining decided non-hag Stella Stevens in *The Mad Room* (1969), Winters was reunited for the "Hansel and Gretel" retelling *Who[ever] Slew Auntie Roo?* (1972) with Harrington. He also cast *Les Diaboliques*' Simone Signoret (*Games*, 1967), *Lady in a Cage* alumna Ann Sothern (*The Killing Kind*, 1973), Gloria Swanson (the TV-movie *Killer Bees*, 2/26/74), and Piper Laurie (*Ruby*, 1977), an Oscar nominee in *Carrie* (1976).

The boundaries being fluid, some of the growing sisterhood fit more neatly in the Farrell mold than others. For Hammer, the deglamorized Tallulah Bankhead terrorized her late son's fiancée (Stefanie Powers) as a *Fanatic* (aka *Die! Die! My Darling!*; 1965), adapted by Matheson from Anne Blaisdell's **Nightmare** (1962), and de Havilland's real sis, Joan Fontaine, tangled with a coven after a breakdown in *The Witches* (aka *The Devil's Own*, 1966). Sibs Reid and Flora Robson hid a dark family secret in Tigon's *The Beast in the Cellar* (1971); Gordon and Bennett — in her final film — had their own evil cults in Roman Polanski's *Rosemary's Baby* (1968) and Dario Argento's *Suspiria* (1977), respectively.

Davis's association with horror in general encompassed the TV-movie *Scream, Pretty Peggy* (11/24/73), miniseries *The Dark Secret of Harvest Home* (1978), and Disney film *The Watcher in the Woods* (1981). Not all homicidal "hags" were played by actual stars, e.g., Mrs. Voorhees (Betsy Palmer) in *Friday the 13th* (1980); conversely, Kathy Bates's Oscar-winning role in the Stephen King adaptation *Misery* (1990) was a breakthrough but Veronica Lake ended her career ignominiously as a Hitler-cloning mad scientist in *Flesh Feast* (1970). Mention must be made of *Mommie Dearest* (1981), based upon Christina Crawford's 1978 autobiography, starring Razzie Award-winning Faye Dunaway as Joan.

Like seemingly everything else, Farrell's best-known work was remade for television, the *raison d'être* for ABC's superfluous *What Ever Happened to Baby Jane?* (2/17/91) presumably being the stunt casting of sisters Vanessa and Lynn Redgrave as Blanche and Jane, respectively. Director David Greene had earned Emmys for *Rich Man, Poor Man* (1976) and *Roots* (1977); scenarist/co-producer Brian Taggert's less prestigious *oeuvre* includes *Poltergeist III* (1988) and the Fox telefilm *Omen IV: The Awakening* (5/20/91). The set-up is basically unchanged, with Blanche crippled as the result of a car crash in which the alcoholic ex-child star Jane — whose success she had eclipsed — allegedly tried to kill her.

Learning of her plans to sell the house, Jane serves a worm sandwich to Blanche, whose physical therapist, Dominick (Bruce A. Young), advises her to have Jane put away. Jane meets the well-named video-store owner and aspiring personal manager Billy Korn (John Glover), who remembers Baby Jane (Samantha Jordon [*sic*]) and offers to help restart her career with a cabaret act recreating the sisters' duet. Hearing Blanche reveal her concern on the phone with Shelby, Jane defuses it with a second call, imitating her voice; she then pretends to serve Blanche a dog belonging to their neighbors, Frank (John Scott Clough) and Connie (Amy Steel) Trotter, into whose yard Blanche tosses a recorded plea for help.

Blanche uncovers evidence of Jane's forgery, falls down the staircase and is tied up when Jane finds the tape in a hedge; Dominick insists on seeing her and is stabbed with scissors by Jane. She is humiliated to learn that the act is a drag revue, with Blanche embodied by Billy, who follows Jane home after she is hooted off the stage and suffers the same fate as Dominick, ironically impaled with an award statuette. Realizing that the jig will soon be up, Jane drives them to the beach, a scene of happy childhood memories, where Blanche, dying of dehydration and starvation, tells the truth about the crash, a brief reconciliation interrupted by the police, who call for help and prevent Jane from walking into the sea . . .

Farrell's influence continued after his death, with the FX miniseries *Feud: Bette and Joan* (2017) chronicling the making of *Baby Jane* and its aftermath; Susan Sarandon, Jessica Lange (in the respective title roles), Alfred Molina (Aldrich), Judy Davis (Hopper), and Stanley Tucci (Jack Warner) all earned Emmy nominations, as did writer-director Ryan Murphy in multiple capacities. Its accuracy was challenged by de Havilland, who — a day before her 101st birthday — filed suit over her portrayal by Catherine Zeta-Jones. But the fact that Farrell's brainchild was the subject of a major production half a century after it was turned into a cult classic leaves his primacy in *Grande Dame Guignol* unquestioned.

• • •

Edition cited: **What Ever Happened to Baby Jane?** (New York: Carroll & Graf, 1991)

FROM OUTER SPACE TO THE WILD WEST
60's Television-to-Comic Book Adaptations
by William Schoell

In the sixties comic book publishers asked themselves: What better way to pander to the sometimes obsessive fans of popular TV shows than by coming out with inexpensive comic book adaptations with all-new stories featuring illustrated versions of the actors? While there were TV-based comic books in the fifties, such as *Captain Video* (which came out from Fawcett in 1951), and in the bronze age (Charlton's *The Six Million Dollar Man*), this article will concentrate on the explosion of titles during the silver age, most of which were published by Dell and Gold Key.

In 1961 Dell comics brought out a one-shot (*Four-Color* 1231) based on the British TV series *Danger Man*, known as *Secret Agent* in America. Patrick McGoohan played

undercover agent John Drake. The comic featured a very suspenseful story wherein various diplomats are being murdered while attending the same traveling circus. Investigating numerous suspects, Drake finally routs the killer before he can bring death to his latest victim. The art by Tony Tallarico features some dramatic full-page panels of a hair-raising roller coaster ride and a pride of lions attacking the killer.

Gold Key then did their own version of the series, calling it *Secret Agent*, in 1966. In the first issue Drake searches for an H-bomb that was jettisoned from a military plane flying over Africa, and also has to deal with enemy agents on the same mission. He winds up on a safari where one by one the participants are murdered in a type of *Ten Little Indians* situation, as Drake even refers to it. *Secret Agent* 2 has Drake pursuing a beautiful freedom-loving dictator's daughter for important tapes that she has in her possession, but she is accompanied by a mammoth bodyguard that Drake finds difficult to bypass. The woman only agrees to turn over the tapes if Drake busts her lover out of her father's prison. Although the TV series was only 30 minutes in length, both issues of the short-lived comic had enough plot for a movie as well as more than decent artwork by Bill Lignante and Bob Jenney.

Gold Key turned the popular series *Voyage to the Bottom of the Sea* into a comic in 1964. The first exciting issue had Admiral Nelson and his wondrous sub The Seaview taking on the challenge of the evil Dr. Gamma, who planned to use his tidal wave machine to blackmail the world. The fourth issue featured the bizarre "Robinson Crusoe of the Depths," in which the Seaview comes across a centuries-old giant living beneath the Sargasso Sea. The kind of story that might have appeared in DC's *Sea Devils*, it was handled with a great deal more intelligence. In "The Great Undersea Safari" in *VBS* 5, a mentally disturbed hunter who lost his nerve tries to redeem himself by hunting Nelson and the Seaview as if it were a huge, deadly beast. It was as much a psychological study as an adventure tale.

VBS 12 presented an alarming tale of what might happen if an intelligent dolphin gained control of the sea's denizens and turned the whole undersea kingdom against mankind, cutting off a major food supply and tying up shipping lanes. The wildest story was in *VBS* 14, in which a fluid from fissures beneath the earth with highly unusual properties so affects the Seaview itself that the submarine grows gills and scales and becomes a *living* creature, even dripping acid so as to *digest* the crew inside it; this was most likely scripted by Dick Wood. There were two more issues of the series after this, but they featured reprints of earlier stories.

The art in *Voyage* — contributed by

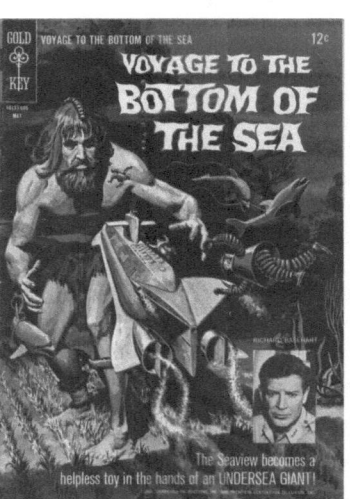

Mike Sekowsky, Don Heck, Alberto Giolitti, George Tuska and others, with striking cover paintings primarily by George Wilson — was of a high order, clean, well-composed, and attractive with some large spectacular panels of the Seaview being tossed about by waves or sailing through gigantic caverns, as well as shots of thrashing blue whales, violent undersea earthquakes and bizarre mutant behemoths. Since there were no budgetary limitations as on the TV show, the writers and artists were free to run wild with their imaginations. The stories in the comic could be fantastic, but never as silly as anything on the TV series. *Voyage to the Bottom of the Sea* was one of the very best television-to-comic adaptations.

Dell came out with a series based on *The Outer Limits* in 1964. Just as the TV series had had to insert monsters into the stories due to network demands regarding ratings, the comic followed the lead, dumbing it down even more. The stories, often apocalyptic, read more like DC sci-fi tales, were on the silly side, and often featured juvenile protagonists. The first issue dealt with aliens that had been taking people and things from earth for decades and finally realize what terror they have been causing when three of these beings are forcibly teleported to earth; an intriguing idea with mediocre results. *OL* 3 presented a suspenseful if unsatisfying tale of an astrophysicist who is convinced his rockets are being sabotaged by gremlins that only he can see.

OL 8 was a variation on *The Blob* when scientists decode a message from outer space, concoct a formula from this code, and find out that aliens have used this method to send a nearly-unkillable, constantly growing lifeform to exterminate everyone on earth. At the end the nations of the world work together, disarm all missiles, and use them to blanket the earth with a cloud that cuts off all sunlight and destroys the blob. This superior issue was like a good B movie. *Outer Limits* 11 presented a harrowing if improbable tale in which a formula that is meant to turn back the evolutionary clock on certain animals only reveals that aliens took the animals' forms centuries ago and said formula turns them back into their monstrous and dangerous original selves.

All of the stories in *Outer Limits* were full-length until the twelfth issue, which contained three tales: a bullied boy gets his revenge when he turns into a giant gillman; an amazing Olympic champion turns out to be a robot; and a vine unleashes green and scaly plant-men. The comic no longer had any resemblance to the TV show but instead ran whimsical stuff you might find in Charlton's fantasy comics. The Japanese monster movie **Rodan** inspired two separate stories! In the amusing "Multiman" in *OL* 13 a crazy professor and a washed-up wrestler team-up as the scientist uses the athlete's body to create dozens of duplicates in order to storm the White House and take over the world. Unfortunately all of the duplicates are linked to the original, and when the wrestler drops dead of a heart attack, they also bite the dust — along with the professor's plans of conquest. The wonderful "Martian Stimulators Inc." in *OL* 14 stars a hen-pecked man who winds up accidentally drinking a cure for baldness that increases his stature both in his physique and in the office, eliciting jealousy in his nasty wife, whose fate is not so marvelous. *OL* 16 features a variation of Hodgson's "The Voice in the Night" set on a space station beset by a fungus-like creature.

Gold Key released a series based on *The Man from U.N.C.L.E.* in 1965. The comic had an auspicious debut with an intelligently-plotted story called "The Explosive Affair,"

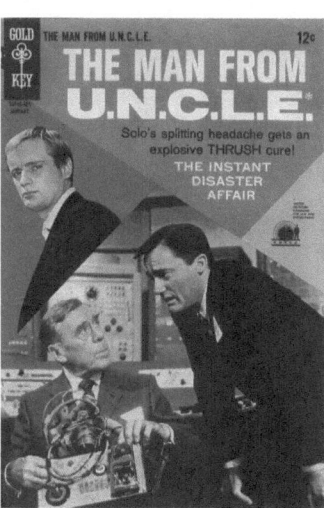

which was beautifully drawn by Don Heck and Mike Esposito for maximum impact. The attention to detail and cinematic approach pulled the reader into the story and the many different locations. "The Rip van Solo Affair" in *MFU* 4 had Napoleon Solo affected by laser radiation during a mission which leaves him susceptible to THRUSH's brain-washing (THRUSH being an evil group intent on world conquest). Before long he is passing out U.N.C.L.E. secrets to an Ilya double and Thrush's ultimate computer, which he eventually destroys. In "The Ten Little Uncles Affair" in *MFU* 5 Napoleon and Ilya race around the world trying to save the lives of ten U.N.C.L.E. agents targeted by THRUSH. In this excellent story THRUSH has built an underwater city from which it plans to gain a stranglehold on shipping lanes.

MFU 8's "The Flying People Affair," in which THRUSH utilizes an anti-gravity paste that makes everything fly off into the air, featured especially good pencils by *Justice League of America* artist Mike Sekowsky. Sekowsky also drew issue 10's "The Trojan Horse Affair," in which a lover of Greek culture named Odysseus schemes to learn U.N.C.L.E.'s secrets and gain entry into THRUSH, only to deal with the latter organization's betrayal. *MFU* 12 had a noteworthy story entitled "The Dead Man's Diary Affair" in which a lower-level THRUSH employee schemes to destroy not U.N.C.L.E. — but THRUSH — in disguise as head man Alexander Waverly.

In *MFU* 14's "The Brain Drain Affair" THRUSH uses a huge and diabolical machine to drain away and absorb all knowledge from the brains of genius scientists. *MFU* 15 features a genuinely clever tale entitled "The Animal Agents Affair," in which THRUSH uses trained animals of all kinds to enact various acts of espionage. They are brought down by, of all things, a flea fitted with "the smallest miniaturized radio bug ever made." Equally unique was *MFU* 16's "The Instant Disaster Affair," in which a scientist unveils a machine which can turn any weapon, no matter how large, into powder for easy, deceptive transport. Adding water to the powder reforms the weapon. "Machines materializing from a powder like instant coffee!" observes Napoleon. Most of the scripts were by Dick Wood and Paul S. Newman.

Gold Key also came out with a *Girl from U.N.C.L.E.* comic book. This, too, had an auspicious debut with "The Fatal Accidents Affair." Frankly, this story of beautiful THRUSH models using a mind-sapping perfume to make saps out of male U.N.C.L.E. agents, causing their "accidental" deaths, was not only entertaining and expertly drawn by Al McWilliams, but better than any episode of the actual TV show; Paul S. Newman was the writer. There was a very exciting scene when U.N.C.L.E. gal April Dancer rescues fellow agent Mark Slate during a daring no-parachute jump, as well as a bevy of beautiful THRUSH villainesses for April to tangle with. *GFU* 2's "The Kid Kommandos' Caper" was another good story about a school mistress who uses her young athletes to carry on the deadly and destructive work of THRUSH. A modern-day Captain Kidd was the villain in *GFU* 3's acceptable story, but by the final two issues the adventures in the comic were just as ludicrous as the ones on the TV show.

Gold Key brought out *The Invaders*, based on the excellent ABC science fiction show in which architect David Vincent tries to warn the world about an outer space invasion, waging a lonely battle against murderous aliens, in 1966. In the first issue, Vincent tries to warn scientists at a radar base about the aliens' sinister interest in them but as usual is rebuffed, then discovers that an alien UFO was hidden behind the illusion of a mountain out in the desert. In the second issue Vincent intervenes when an Air Force Major is mind-controlled by the aliens, going so far as to try to commit sabotage and even murder his own little boy, who's seen too much. "The Moon Tilters" in *Invaders* 3 has the aliens plotting to wipe out the world's inhabitants with massive planet-wide flooding until Vincent and some allies race against time to open a dam and destroy the infernal device causing the rising waters.

The fourth issue had two excellent stories. In "The Doomsday Window," Vincent and his colleague Edgar Scoville manage to grab a device, a circular hoop, from the aliens which the latter desperately want returned to them. The hoop turns out to be a dimension warp that, upon being enlarged, can bring the aliens' ships across the galaxies with even greater speed and in greater numbers than before. In "Rendezvous at Grizzly Mesa" an alien named Primus reveals that he and others like him want to remain on Earth and live free, and are willing to fight off the invasion along with Vincent and Scoville. The pair manage to enlist the aid of a general who doesn't believe them until he sees one of the alien craft for himself and becomes another ally. Unfortunately *The Invaders* only lasted for four issues, failing to survive past the cancellation of the series, which ran for two years. The stories were as good as the ones on the TV show, and Dan Spiegle's art was adept and attractive.

Honey West, based on the ABC-TV series about a lady private eye, had one issue brought out by Gold Key in 1966; this contained two stories. The first has Honey guarding a yacht party from jewel thieves but coming up against traders of government secrets instead, while the second has her investigating why a boxer is constantly being threatened into taking a dive. Jack Sparling's art was adequate but rushed, and the stories were no great shakes.

Another short-lived 1966 TV adaptation from Gold Key was *The Green Hornet*, a character that had originally appeared on the radio, in movie serials, and in comic books before getting the television treatment after the success of the campy *Batman; The Hornet*, however, was played straight. Britt Reid was a newspaper publisher who took after criminals in the guise of the Green Hornet with his butler/ bodyguard Kato at his side driving their souped-up car, Black Beauty. One of Reid's reporters, Mike Axford, was convinced the Hornet was a crook himself, unaware that Reid worked with District Attorney Scanlon, who knew his secret identity. The first issue has the Hornet tackling a villain who uses a drug to force people to obey his commands and then forget they ever saw him.

In an exciting story in *Green Hornet* 2, he and Kato smash a protection racket run by a gang calling itself the Red Dragons, the chief enforcer of which uses a massive flame thrower against his enemies. In the third issue, the Hornet and Kato first save a wealthy boy prince from abductors, and then tackle a duo of imposters in similar garb at a charity masquerade ball who try to make off with the booty. The comic, although it only lasted three issues, was superior to the rather bland TV show and boasted excellent Dan Spiegle visuals.

Dell came out with a *Mission: Impossible* comic book in 1967. In the first issue, Dan Briggs leads the squad in two stories. The first employs only two regular members of the team, Briggs and Barney, as well as a female skydiver named Dina and an underwater diver named Sandy; the mission — to recover camera footage taken by a reconnaissance plane of a Communist-

held island. The second story, "The Deadly Defector," was more exciting, as Cinnamon joins the other two men to secure a Chinese physicist who wants to defect.

Mission: Impossible 2 has the team trying to recover a list of double-agents that is hidden on a mountain precipice behind the iron curtain. Joining Briggs, Cinnamon and Willy is a character named Connet, a sea rescue specialist, who just happens to look like disguise master Rollin Hand. In one improbable scene Cinnamon sails across a pulley to the mountain and digs for the list in the icy snow *without wearing gloves*, which might account for her "nearly frozen fingers." The second story has the team smuggling a bacteriologist onto an island so that he can destroy cultures to be used in bacteriological warfare; this fairly good story has Barney tackling an octopus and killing it with his knife.

The lead story in *Mission: Impossible* 3 has the team challenged to discover if a NATO missile base is really as impregnable as it seems. In the second story a doctor is smuggled into an iron curtain prison to give an arrested American attache a drug to counter the effects of his communist brainwashing. By the time the fourth issue was published, Peter Graves as Jim Phelps had replaced Steven Hill as Dan Briggs on the show, but while Graves appears on the cover and his face is used for the stories inside, the other characters call him "Dan." The first story in the issue was as good as anything on the series, as Cinnamon enters the Trans-Europe racing competition so she can switch places *during the race* with a another woman driver who wants to defect and is being pursued by enemy agents. Complicating matters is another driver whose car conceals smuggled gold bars. The MI team could be pretty ruthless on the TV show, but in the issue's second story they actually hijack an airliner as part of a plot to get a kidnapped American official off of an island similar to Cuba.

Steven Hill was back on the cover of *Mission: Impossible* 5, but only because it was a reprint of the first issue. Considering that the TV show ran for seven years, the comic book should have had a lengthy run, but despite some creditable stories the series never caught on. The art was serviceable, if somewhat crude. Although Rollin Hand appeared in some of the stories, he never used his powers of disguise. Had another publisher secured the rights, they might not have muffed it the way Dell did.

In 1967 Gold Key did an adaptation of the popular post-Civil War spy show *The Wild, Wild West*, in which two secret service agents — James West and Artemus Gordon — working for President Grant, travel around the country (via a special, richly-appointed custom railroad train) uncovering nefarious plots and antagonists. In the first issue, a desperado takes over several small western towns, trains men in everything from gun-slinging to horse-stealing, and amasses a large private cavalry to turn himself into the ruler of his own dynasty. In the second issue, the boys deal with a descendant of Napoleon who decides to get back the Louisiana territory that Bonaparte sold to the U.S. for a pittance and mesmerizes men into doing his bidding for him from his electrified HQ in New Orleans.

WWW 3 features an excellent story in which the boys guard a Russian duke who wants to hunt in Cheyenne territory, but who turns out to be a phony after their land and the petroleum that lies underneath. Then there was a phony Montezuma to whom they are nearly sacrificed [*WWW* 4]; another phony who pretends to be the executed Emperor Maximilian and uses blimps to attack military trains and raid weapons caches [6]; the nefarious, deceptive Madame Shanghai, who kidnaps the nephew of the Chinese Emperor [5]; and Captain Hawke, who commands a submarine that uses giant hooks to scoop treasure from shipwrecks at the sea bottom [7].

One difference between the TV show and the comic was that in the latter everyone seemed to think that James West was an idle millionaire who spent his time sightseeing and basically doing nothing, but on the TV show West and Gordon never hid the fact that they were secret service agents unless they were on an undercover assignment. The comic only lasted 7 issues but it was nearly as much fun as the TV series.

The original series of *Star Trek*, which lasted three seasons in the 1960's, was turned into a comic by at least three different companies: Gold Key, Marvel and DC. Gold Key's *Star Trek* series debuted in 1967 and lasted a lot longer than the TV series. The first issue had a lively if somewhat absurd tale called "Planet of No Return" with the Enterprise crew battling against a variety of intelligent and often carnivorous fauna. The second issue was more down to earth but also had a good idea: the Enterprise investigates an asteroid that holds prisoners who are condemned to die when the asteroid blows up, although they have no idea when that might occur.

"The Haunted Asteroid" in *ST* 19 is an intriguing tale of a planetoid that has been made into a shrine for a dead princess (the three-quarter page panel by Alberto Giolitti and Sal Trapani depicting this shrine is quite striking) but now is said to be haunted by the ghosts of those who tried to loot the treasures that were placed in the shrine. *ST* 22's "Siege in Superspace" [1974] introduces a bio-mechanical menace — botanical-mechanical might be a better term for it as the creature is composed of both vegetable and metallic parts — 3 years before *Alien*.

With the thirtieth issue the once-attractive art underwent a change and the series generally lost its visual gloss, although there were still some marvelous painted covers, some issues still had solid inside art jobs, and there were still some good scripts. ST 33 had the Enterprise heading toward the section of space where the "big bang" that created the universe was said to originate and encountering another James Kirk who claims to come from the universe that existed before ours. The two men wind up fighting a duel to the death, but when our Kirk does not kill the earlier one, he is told that he has made the right choice. The story (by Al Moniz) has a lot of intriguing elements, even if it doesn't quite go anywhere, and even Captain Kirk wonders if the whole thing even happened.

ST 41 was a superior issue with an excellent story by Arnold "Doom Patrol" Drake and first-rate work by Al McWilliams, an artist who made the characters resemble recognizable human beings and not cartoon characters. In "The Evictors" the Enterprise crew celebrate the 10,000ᵗʰ year of recorded history of the planet Nraka with its rulers. These people have always worshiped a legendary being called Zotar. To their surprise a huge spaceship arrives containing a race of beings, the Soonora, whose appearance is similar to Zotar's. Unfortunately, an emissary from the ship tells them that they were the original inhabitants of Nraka who had to flee due to a natural disaster. Now, half a million years later, they have returned and want their planet back. If the current Nrakians do not leave within a prescribed time, they will be destroyed. Dvor, who rules Nraka, thinks that the Soonorians are phonies, mere space pirates, and Kirk is inclined to agree. Still, he tries to remain neutral, yet finally admits that if it were Earth he wouldn't give up without a fight. The Nrakains (most of whom have

declared that their "god [Zotar] is dead" and are rioting against all foreigners) and the Soonorians engage in bloody warfare, until the latter are routed and disappear. Then a shocked Kirk discovers that their story was actually true . . . The tragedy is that if the Soonorians had suggested a compromise the conflict might have been avoided and they might have regained at least a portion of their home planet.

The last two years or so of issues were all drawn by Al McWilliams, who seemed to get better and better at it, turning in some highly satisfactory art jobs, with most of the scripting handled by George Kashdan. Kashdan contributed a creepy tale in ST 56 with Kirk and Spock trying to reverse the negative effects that a mad dictator's trip back to the days of Hannibal had on the future/present universe, as well as an exciting story in ST 58 in which Kirk and company have to rid a giant brain growing inside a planet of the virus that's driving the people on the surface insane. The series ended in 1979 with its 61st issue in which Harry Mudd tries pulling a con on some Klingons.

Last and least, in 1968 Gold Key came out with one issue of The Avengers, based on the British tongue-in-cheek spy program that played on ABC in the U.S. Because the Marvel super-hero comic of that title already existed, the cover featured the words "John Steed" and "Emma Peel" — the two main characters — in big letters and referred to the TV series in smaller letters below. The two stories inside held none of the charm and little of the excitement of that series' best episodes and were poorly drawn as well. In the first there is a plot to hire foreign spies as actors, and the second deals with a machine that can create realistic mirages over the countryside. Mercifully there was no Avengers 2.

• • •

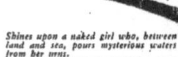

THE POWER OF STANTON CARLISLE
Nightmare Alley and the Cost of Censorship
by J. Charles Burwell

"It was the dark alley, all over again. With a light at the end of it. Ever since he was a kid Stan had had the dream. He was running down a dark alley, the buildings vacant and black and menacing on either side. Far down at the end of it, a light burned; but there was something behind him, close behind him, getting closer until he woke up trembling and never reached the light . . . a nightmare alley."

" . . . can control anybody by finding out what he's afraid of . . . Think out things most people are afraid of and hit them right where they live . . . Fear is the key to human nature . . . Fear. Find out what they are afraid of and sell it back to them. That's the key."

"I'm a hustler, God damn it . . . I'm on the make. Nothing matters in this goddamned lunatic asylum of a world but dough. When you get that you're the boss. If you don't have it you're the end man on the daisy chain . . . I'm going to milk it out of those chumps and take them for the gold in their teeth before I'm through."

William Lindsay Gresham's original novel, **Nightmare Alley**, is some kind of black-hearted epic and study in corruption, tracing the rise and fall of one Stanton Carlisle; from carny hustler to high society medium to aimless fugitive, ultimately sinking into depths borne of his own fear and self-loathing. Beginning in the hardscrabble world of itinerant 1930s carnivals, Carlisle learns the mind-reading trade, becoming a first-rate "mentalist"; scamming the hungry and innocent for their hard-earned cash, and opening up their innermost hopes and fears. Not content with the easy-pickings of small town carnival goers, Carlisle eventually takes his act on the road, becoming "Stanton the Great" and plying his trade in fancy ballrooms and exclusive parties. His turning point occurs when he decides to expand his entertainments into something more serious (and dangerous); the "spook racket," or spiritualism. He uses increasingly elaborate gimmickry to convince his rich marks that he can communicate with loved ones who have passed on to the afterlife. Laying bare their emotions and yearnings of years past, Carlisle eventually gets in too deep and is exposed for the charlatan that he is. He takes it on the lam and sinks into a morass of alcohol-fueled paranoia, hiding out in cheap hotels and hobo jungles. At

19

the end of the novel, he comes full-circle and returns to carnival life, no longer a young man on the make, but, instead, a haunted and fearful shadow.

At a glance, this may sound like a simple fast-moving tale of a confidence man. But Gresham layers it with Carlisle's compulsions and torturous memories, all of which function as chinks in his armor of cynicism and contempt. We learn that, as a child, he witnessed his mother's sexual tryst with a piano teacher. To make matters worse, she engages him in covering up her infidelity by lying to his suspicious father. Ironically, she rewards him for this conspiracy with the gift of a coveted professional magician's kit, setting the stage for both his performance career and his nascent corruption.

In another flashback, we learn that his mother has run away with her lover, leaving him behind with his bitter and violent father. Both the young Carlisle and his beloved dog, Gyp, become victims of the father's sadistic beatings. Tellingly, and throughout the novel, Carlisle has tense encounters with middle-aged men who have the beginnings of gray stubble along their jaws

and chin, as did his father. This invariably sets him off into a swirl of resentment and rage, all fueling his outwardly cool and fraudulent manipulations. As later parts of the novel depict his downward spiral, he is no longer able to maintain his control and he becomes unhinged, slipping into moments of sudden brutality.

Carlisle's psychological debris impacts his relationships with women, particularly with three of the most sharply-drawn characters in the novel. There is Zeena, the veteran carny, who knowingly teaches him the mind-reading racket while cheerfully relieving him of his virginity. For a while, Carlisle hungers both for her body and for the skill with which she gets over on

the rubes and rednecks gathered around her platform. Carlisle learns what he can and then his eyes begin to wander, finally settling on Molly, a young woman who somehow maintains her innocence amid the sordid trappings of carnival life. She gives herself to him after he saves her from a police raid and they leave the carnival together, taking their act on the road. She becomes his wife and partner in an even slicker scam, they perform as "mentalists" for rich swells in nightclubs, mansions, and fancy hotels. Initially, she is reluctant to become part of his new "spook racket." For her, the notion of contacting the dead goes far beyond the simple realm of carnival fakery, and, along with its religious trappings, is a moral line she doesn't want to cross. There's a sheer level of cruelty and blasphemy to it. Carlisle has no such scruples; for him it's the big time, it means a lot more dough and also a chance to put something over on the arrogant upper classes. The turning point comes when, after a mind-reading performance, he is handed a note from their wealthy hostess directing him and Molly not to mingle with her guests. This enrages Carlisle and he becomes even more determined to manipulate the rich and drain them of their money and dignity. He convinces Molly that spiritualism is their ticket to a better life, and so, with much misgiving, she poses as the Reverend Carlisle's medium, his ostensible vessel to the afterlife.

And then there is Dr. Lilith Ritter, the third lover in Carlisle's life, and something else altogether. As the psychotherapist for many in the society set, she has a direct connection to the people Carlisle is eager to victimize. Her professional office is filled with complete files and recordings of her sessions, all of which contain accounts of her clientele's secrets, misdeeds, and perversions. Quickly understanding the nature of Carlisle's game, she insinuates herself into his life and becomes his collaborator, lover, and analyst. She begins feeding him sensitive information about her patients, which he uses to convince his marks of his spiritual powers and ethereal communication with their departed beloved. Chief among these is one Ezra Grindle, an elderly millionaire who harbors an obsessive guilt over Dorrie, a past love from his youth, long dead from a fatal abortion. Carlisle becomes deeply involved with Grindle and his need for forgiveness, all of which foments tragic and dangerous consequences.

Meanwhile, the calculatingly seductive Dr. Ritter is having "therapy" sessions with Carlisle, slowly eliciting his sordid past, and facilitating his growing anxiety and invidious fears. Even though he continues to use Molly as an integral part of his "spook racket," he is losing interest in her as a wife. He's plainly in thrall to the ice queen Ritter and acknowledges that she has some kind of "golden thread to his brain."

Framing the novel, and its depiction of Carlisle's rise and fall, is the image of the "Geek." In contrast to its 1980s connotation of an awkwardly unattractive computer nerd, a carnival geek of the '30s and '40s represented the lowest kind of attraction those traveling shows had to offer. A far-gone filthy alcoholic is kept in a cage or pit, his only subsistence the chickens or snakes with which he seemingly (or actually) bites off their heads. His reward for such degradation is a bottle a day and a place to safely sleep it off. Author Gresham first heard of this human anomaly from a fellow veteran of the Spanish Civil War while both were waiting to return home. The image of the Geek haunted him, and he transferred that obsession to his fictional creation. It becomes a telling and key part of Carlisle's journey down Nightmare Alley.

For its time (published by Rinehart in 1946), **Nightmare Alley** surely pulled no punches in its hardscrabble tone and its open depiction of sex, alcoholism and sordid perversion. This was offensive to some reviewers then, as was the raw language found in the narrative and spoken dialogue. And yet, at the same time, the story and its characters are so compelling that it remains a veritable page-turner of a novel, even for jaded readers in 2022. Besides the tale's unexpected turn of events, there are life-lessons to be had about the gray areas between good and evil, and the danger of misplaced faith.

These contrasting aspects were borne out by some of its contemporary reviews in printed media, as well as its eventual censorship in subsequent editions. The following quotes from various newspapers are instructive:

Ray Gould, in the *Montgomery Advertiser*, 9/29/46: "*this profoundly shocking and evil novel has a strong moral but it will take readers with strong stomachs to read through the often vulgar, often obscene, dark doings which are printed between the covers of this danse macabre.*"

William Targ in the *Philadelphia Inquirer*, 9/8/46: "*Despite the ugliness and horror inherent in this novel, its honesty cannot be challenged, nor its artistry.*"

Ralph Looney in the *Lexington Herald-Leader*, 9/8/46: "*Brutally Realistic novel of Seamy Side of Life Probably Will Rate Boston Ban . . . the work unquestionably will create much discussion and controversy.*"

WM in the *Boston Globe*, 9/11/46: "*Somehow it seems the author could have captured the earthy authenticity of 'carny folks' without resorting to the crude language of the gutter. Whatever was gained in unique plot development appears to have been dissipated by the wanton use of pornography.*"

Wes Keeler in *The Post-Star* (Glen Falls, NY), 9/28/46: "*It hardly seems possible that a more ugly story could be conceived.*"

Florence Fisher-Parry in *The Pittsburgh Press*, 11/11/46: "*There are things that people of taste just omit . . . Are there no longer any unmentionables in conversation, in drama and in fiction? . . . fairly well-written but thoroughly abhorrent to normal healthy tastes . . . the most degrading excursion I have ever taken through the cesspools of fiction.*"

Benjamin Howder in *The Los Angeles Times*, 9/15/46: "* . . . this sardonic, brilliant, and constantly unexpected novel is destined to be a great best seller. It will also be pounced upon by yellow journalists and their stooges amongst purity legions; and after the trial is over and the book vindicated of filth charges it will outsell itself . . . a novel without a solitary dull moment . . . shocking in frankness and needfully so . . . "

And, as it turned out, **Nightmare Alley** was censored. Today's readers fortunately have the 2010 New York Review Books edition, which adheres to the novel as originally issued in 1946. Comparing it to the 1949 Signet paperback edition (issued just a few years after the original hardcover and featuring wonderful cover art by James Avati) reveals a number of modifications and sheer cuts to the novel's language:

In "Card 12, The Star," "*I was screwing her on the side*" becomes "*I was sleeping with her on the side*" in the '49 edition. And " *. . . society dames with the clap, bankers that take it up the ass . . .* " becomes "*society dames with a dose, bankers that have fishy eyes . . .* "

In "Card 14, The Tower," Carlisle tells Grindle, "*All you wanted was a piece of ass!,*" which becomes "*All you wanted was a girl!*"

In "Card 17, The Hermit," Carlisle is talking to some fellow hobos " *. . . How would you like it if we had an unexpected guest? . . . He'd find us in a dither, it being the maid's day off. All we'd have to offer him would be a drink of that fine mellow, wood-aged polecat piss.*" In the '49 Signet edition, the last line is completely cut out.

And, in "Card 19, The Wheel of Fortune," a black hobo tells Carlisle, "*What's the matter with having a little poontang? Nothing dirty about that except in a crib you likely get crabs or a dose.*" This passage is completely eliminated in the '49 Signet.

Apparently, this kind of censorship of the novel persisted for years, possibly until the NYRB version finally came out. On the other hand, what should be pointed out is that the cuts made were *language*-related.

The events, characterizations, and power of the narrative remained, despite the censorship. This writer's first encounter with the novel was the Signet paperback and it made a deep impression, even with what was later to be discovered as much tamer verbiage than the original edition.

Not long after its publication, the novel **Nightmare Alley** was read by Hollywood actor Tyrone Power, who convinced 20th Century Fox mogul, Darryl Zanuck to purchase its rights for film production. Power, who had been relegated to, what was for him, a tiresome succession of leading man or action roles, wanted to expand his performing range with an atypical vehicle he could sink his teeth into. The novel's clever sociopath, Stanton Carlisle, was made to order for such an experiment.

Some time prior to its release, the novel's purchase by Fox was noted by Jimmy Fidler of *The Capital Times* (Madison, Wisconsin, 10/10/46): "*20th Century Fox has purchased screen rights to* **Nightmare Alley** *. . . since neither the Johnston Office nor the various state and municipal censors could permit the exhibition of a picture faithfully adhering to the plot . . . it follows that studio bosses plan a complete rewriting job.*"

We'll probably never know whether Fidler's last statement is factual or simply his opinion (any research on this point would be very welcome). But given the routine censorship of American films during the era, it certainly is understandable. As a reaction to the perceived excesses of moving pictures, particularly in regard to sex, violence, and society's moral order (and the resulting fear of a commercial boycott), the movie industry put a rigid production code into place, one that governed the content of each and every picture to be released. The Motion Picture Production Code functioned from 1934 until 1968 (when the now-familiar rating system was first developed), and specifically dictated what was acceptable and unacceptable in a film's plot, theme, and action. Initially, its most famous arbiter was Joseph Breen, who enforced the code through the Hays office of the Motion Picture Association of America.

Every film had to have the Hays office's approval before it could be distributed to theaters and the moral standards of its viewers. Of course, this included Fox' production of *Nightmare Alley*, which came out in the Fall of 1947. On first glance, there would be a lot to censor in transforming the novel into a suitable film. Among others, the Code's dictates included: No ridicule of the clergy or the forces of law and order, no sympathy for a criminal (their actions always had to be punished), and no depiction of seduction or men and women in bed together. Sex outside of marriage was never to be presented as something that was positive and desirable. Additionally, there was to be no depiction of overt "brutality or gruesomeness."

Film-makers of the 1940's, particularly those that were producing what was later called film noir, had to find subtle and clever ways to present stories of crime and sexual transgression. They had to be able to plumb the darkness while appearing to adhere to the Code's rules. Many films noir were approved in this manner and *Nightmare Alley* is no exception.

As released in the Fall of '47, the picture was scripted by Jules Furthman and directed by Edmund Goulding. Headlined by Power as Stanton Carlisle, the film also featured Joan Blondell as Zeena, Coleen Gray as the youthful Molly, and Helen Walker as the ultimately duplicitous Lilith Ritter. They all give bravura performances and Carlisle's rise and fall is told with verve and a compelling narrative. The depiction of the novel's key events is unchanged; what is left out is the rawness of the language and the frank descriptions of sex and brutality. Instead, those elements take place off-screen; they may be heard but not seen, or they simply may be described

through the characters' dialogue.

In the opening scene of the film, we see Power as Stanton Carlisle, standing with a crowd watching the Geek. We never see the pitiful creature, his nature is revealed through a conversation Stanton has with his boss: *"How do you get that way? Are you born that way?"* We only hear the Geek, and more directly, see the fascination and horror he evokes, in Stan's face and in those of the carnival-goers surrounding him.

True to the Code and its restrictions, there is no open depiction of sexuality in the '47 version of '**Alley**. The novel's detailed flashbacks of Stan observing his mother's infidelity and eventual abandonment are completely absent. At the film's beginning, it is assumed he is already an experienced young man, and not the callow virgin we see openly described in Gresham's writing. His affairs with the women in his life are alluded to in subtle ways; After Carlisle

"saves" Molly from being arrested by a zealous lawman, they kiss and declare their attraction to each other. But Molly looks at him, and asks what about him and Zeena? He quickly denies that there is anything between them, he only wants the system of verbal cues and signals that Zeena and her husband Pete developed for their mind-reading act. Following this scene, Stan and Molly rejoin their fellow carnies. The strongman Bruno, who himself is smitten with Molly, suspiciously tells her he was looking for her, where did she go? Contemptuously, she fires back at him, *"Where do you think I was?"* The perceptive viewer will know that she and Stan have just had a tryst, (although in keeping with the Code, it is not stated bluntly). Bruno, Zeena, and the other carnies know this as well, and force the two to marry each other in a shotgun-style wedding.

The other element in which the '47 film worked around the code was in its references to the law and established religion. In one of the movie's turning points, a local sheriff and his deputies raid the carnival and threaten to close it down. Staring at Molly with both lust and disgust, he wants to arrest her for "indecent exposure." (As part of her act, she wears a flimsy outfit with lamé appliques that look like hands covering her breasts). He also wants to collar the Geek which, he tells them, is an "illegal act." Carlisle quickly sizes up the cop and "reads" him; talking to him gently while bringing up his standing in the community, his time in church, and the *"love of a good woman . . . don't hate your enemies, forgive them."* Apparently mollified by Carlisle's soft-soap, the sheriff quiets down and leaves without arresting anyone. On the surface, he has been treated with the respect due to his position. But, after he is gone, Stan comments to Molly about his success in manipulating him: *"It was a lead pipe."* Molly responds by sneering, *"that old hypocrite."*

Later on in the scene, Zeena asks Stan how he could talk so knowledgeably about religion. He tells her he learned that "stuff" in an orphanage and reform school. He got in good with its chaplain, who "saved" him when he got in trouble. *"Salvation comes in handy when you're in a jam."* After hearing him wax so poetically to the sheriff about a little country church and its choir, it is startling to hear that religion is just another piece of his carny tool kit. The message is a subversive one and was apparently lost on the denizens of the Hays office.

On the other hand, as the film moves towards its climax, Molly suddenly becomes fearful and conscience-stricken, particularly with her role in Stanton's "spook racket." As part of the scam he's running on Ezra Grindle, he wants Molly to "materialize" and appear as the millionaire's long-lost love. She is aghast at this proposition and wants to draw the line, an openly religious one. "*You're going against God.*" She points out that he is talking like he's a minister, but, "*You're not talking to one of your chumps, you're talking to me, who knows you red, white, and blue.*" But she reluctantly agrees to the ruse, and Stanton continues to work on Grindle, who confesses, "*Because of the life I've led, I don't know much about God.*" Ultimately, Molly can't go through with it and Stanton's carefully laid plans hit the proverbial fan.

Molly and Stanton Carlisle are central characters in this narrative, and their views on law and religion range from contempt to ambiguity. The expression of those views certainly didn't conform to the Production Code but were subtle enough for the film to be approved for release. It also helped that Carlisle is not rewarded in life, quite the opposite. Nevertheless, one can only wonder what the movie's audience felt at the time and if they secretly identified with his temporary victories or left the theater satisfied with his inevitable demise.

Flash forward to 2021. A newly filmed version of **Nightmare Alley** arrives, unencumbered by the long discarded Production Code and benefiting from years of movie productions that ranged from frank to uninhibited in their depictions of sex and violence. A knowledgeable viewer might think that any new version of the novel would take its cue from the uncensored edition released in 2010. There would be no need to dance around Stanton's trysts, his sordid past, or the sudden violence he precipitates. The events could be portrayed in all of their grim and fascinating detail, while still adhering to the arc of Carlisle's spectacular rise and fall. As a noir fable, **Nightmare Alley**'s bleak lessons could be presented without any filter and to a contemporary audience, many of whom were accustomed to (if not demanding of) a cinema experience that was akin to watching a train wreck.

As directed by Guillermo del Toro, who also penned the screenplay with Kim Morgan, 2021's *Nightmare Alley* comes packaged as a retro-fitted modern day thriller, complete with an "R" rating. The explanation for such is listed as "Strong/ Bloody Violence, Some Sexual Content, Nudity, and Language." This latest version has all of that, yet it still presents the essential plot of the novel and the '47 film: Stanton Carlisle (as played by Bradley Cooper) joins a wandering carnival, becomes a first-rate mentalist, hits the big time, and deliberately insinuates himself into the dangerous "spook racket." He crosses the moral line constantly; he has affairs with three women, provides a fatal bottle to Pete, Zeena's husband, and manipulates others' grief and longing for his own profit. And it all ultimately leads to his downfall and a life that is without a shred of aspiration or hope.

However, del Toro (and presumably Morgan) has taken the character of Carlisle and invested him with a greater degree of pathology than is seen in Tyrone Power's portrayal or even in the novel's conception. His mother's affair and elopement with the piano teacher, which is excruciatingly detailed in the novel, merits only a mention in del Toro's film. Carlisle shares only a fragment of the story when he is under "analysis" with the duplicitous Lilith Ritter (played by Cate Blanchett). Instead, del Toro frequently returns to the scene that begins the film; Carlisle is seen inside a dilapidated house, dragging an enshrouded body into a pit and then torching it. He leaves the burning house to catch a bus out of town and eventually gets off at the carnival. In subsequent flashbacks, the scene is repeated and then progressively expanded to show him sitting closely by an old man's bedside, whispering to him inaudibly. At one point, we even see him lounging in the middle of the house while it goes up in flames around him. Until the end of the film, it is unclear what is real about this scenario and what is his own fantasy. When its explication is finally revealed, and seen in light of his other actions, it shows that Carlisle is more than just a silver-tongued con-man, he actually is capable of real violence.

And violence permeates the del Toro version of *Nightmare Alley*, through actual events in the film, as well as by the characters' revelations and disclosures. Besides Carlisle himself, there is the ominous figure of Ezra Grindle, (played by Richard Jenkins). In the '47 film, he is presented as a personage of refinement and outward gentility. It is easy to think that his confession of a Godless life has more to do with the simple pursuit of wealth and position than with anything that was blatantly sinful. Del Toro's Grindle, on the other hand, is decidedly sinister. Grey-bearded and suspiciously taciturn, he is surrounded by lawyers and thuggish bodyguards. While waiting for the "materialization" of his beloved Dorrie, he chillingly confesses to Carlisle that *"I've done things I never told anyone about, . . . I've hurt many other women . . . rid my soul of anger . . . I hurt them."* When he suddenly discovers how Carlisle has manipulated his innermost and cherished emotions, he reacts rapidly and brutally.

This is foreshadowed in Carlisle's earlier encounters with Dr. Ritter. As they plot their collaboration, he brings up millionaire Grindle as an obvious "mark." The normally unflappable therapist visibly shudders at this suggestion, telling Carlisle that there would be

consequences for such a move, Grindle is *"unstable, unpredictable."* Lilith is scared and reluctant to say anything more than that. Instead, she slowly unfolds her dress, revealing a long hideous scar running from her breasts and down past her navel. The implication of this is clear but Carlisle is unfazed; he tenderly kisses the scar, almost cementing their devious relationship (Earlier, he has told her, *"I know you're no good and neither am I"*). But, later, he steals her recorded files on Grindle and learns about the abortion, the man's malfeasance, and his guilt. Despite her warnings, he is determined to go through with the con.

This kind of foreshadowing runs throughout del Toro's film, in both obvious and subtle ways. Carlisle is frequently warned about the dangers of spiritualism and even the excesses that come with "mind reading." In an early scene, Carlisle is learning the racket from veteran carny Pete and is fascinated by the cherished book of verbal cues that Pete and Zeena used for years to rope in the suckers. But, Pete, admittedly flawed but nonetheless wiser, warns the younger man about its pitfalls: *"You never do a spook show . . . This book can be misused, that's why I stopped . . . believing your own lies. No man can outrun God. People get hurt, you lie, you lie!"* Waiting for Pete to finally pass out, Carlisle unsuccessfully attempts to steal the book. But after Pete's death, it's finally given to him by Zeena who, knowing that Carlisle is a born "reader," tells him that he's earned it. As events unfold in the film, it will become clear that he will pay for it, as well.

Throughout all three versions of this sordid tale, the images of traditional Tarot fortune-telling cards are used to illustrate

Carlisle's mind-set and to reveal his ultimate downfall. In Gresham's novel, he employs the deck's "Major Arcana" as chapter headings; it begins with "Card I, The Fool" and moves on to, variously, "Card III, The High Priestess," "Card XIX, The Wheel of Fortune," ending with "Card XXII, The Hanged Man." Each card proves to be symbolic of an event or character in the story. In the '47 film, Zeena casually introduces the Tarot to Carlisle; it's just another con in her bag of tricks. Her playful attitude quickly turns sober when she unwittingly draws the Death card and then The Hanged Man. Both cards are portents of disaster and, shortly after this scene, Carlisle inadvertently passes the poisonous bottle of wood alcohol to Pete. This serves to end the older man's life and career while opening the door to Carlisle's own. And later on, (as depicted in both films), Carlisle and Molly have hit the big time and are paid a visit by their old carnival cronies, Zeena, Bruno, and the Major. Molly is happy to see them, Stan not so much. As they party, Zeena pulls out her Tarot deck and begins laying it out, one card at a time. One card drops on the floor. It's The Hanged Man again and Zeena, suddenly frightened, looks at Carlisle and echoes Pete's warning; *"Don't do the spook show!"* He doesn't want to hear this and he angrily throws them out. The party is over, and in more ways than one.

For fans of dark suspense and aficionados of edgy crime fiction, one would be hard-pressed to find a more compelling story than Stanton Carlisle's journey in **Nightmare Alley.** They might wonder about which version to start with. The tightly-written novel is rich in detail and has a depth of characterization that is not always possible in other mediums. It provides insights into the background and motivations of Carlisle, Molly, and even some of the more transient figures in the carnival setting. There is also more technical detail about the mechanics and equipment that help foster the illusions in seances and mind-reading acts. Besides being able to reveal the potential callousness and evil in human hearts, William Lindsay Gresham also portrayed a range of settings; from the gritty underbelly of carnival life to the pining emptiness behind the rich glitterati.

The '47 film is rightly considered one of the classics of mid-century film noir, albeit an unconventional one. Tightly directed and with an evocative setting, both in sunshine and shadow, it also contains what often is viewed as Tyrone Power's finest performance. A Hollywood-mandated glimmer of hope at its conclusion can't hide the darkness and decay that breathes at its core.

As for del Toro's 2021 vision, anecdotal discussions (both actual and virtual) seem to reveal a divided audience response. People seem to either like it or summarily dismiss it. It is apparent that some of the criticism stems from comparing it to the '47 version. And despite garnering an Oscar nomination for Best Picture, it apparently didn't overwhelm at the box office. But, for this writer, it's a tour de force. One first has to mention the vivid art direction and set design. The carnival scenes are colorful and dynamic, and laden with hidden clues about Carlisle and his ultimate fate. The scenes with the Geek are raw and uncensored, as is the final dance between the con-man and rich mark Ezra Grindle. Bradley Cooper plays Carlisle as both slick and vulnerable, a would-be winner who just can't get out of his own way. Cate Blanchett plays Dr. Ritter like some kind of seductive snake; you can't take your eyes off her. She does justice to Helen Walker's equally chilling performance in the earlier Power vehicle. Although del Toro has crafted a two and half hour epic, it didn't seem nearly so long to this writer, even with repeated viewings.

This writer's advice? Read the novel first (the 2010 unexpurgated edition) and see both films, each of which stand on their own merits. On the other hand, you could enter this story in any order, in any configuration. If you're a fan of the darkness, (even if it's at a safe distance), you'll enjoy it. And you certainly won't forget it any time soon.

• • •

(Much thanks to Fred Burwell for his assistance with the research for this article.)

Science Fiction

26061/$1.50

a novel by **GEORGE LUCAS**

STAR WARS

FROM THE ADVENTURES OF **LUKE SKYWALKER**

ALWAYS IN MOTION, THE FUTURE IS
Forty-five Years of *Star Wars* Expanded Universe Fiction
by Jay Shepard

In the beginning was the word, and the word was "*Another galaxy, another time.*" These were the first words printed in the Prologue for the original novelization of *Star Wars*, which kicked-off more than 45 years of *Star Wars* literature. Emerging in December 1976, **Star Wars: From the Adventures of Luke Skywalker** broke all sales records months before the film was released in May 1977. This innocent paperback, which featured cover art by *Star Wars* concept-artist Ralph McQuarrie, was attributed to author George Lucas, sold for a mere $1.50, and first introduced readers to the fantastic world in a galaxy "far, far away..." It was a smash success, selling its first print run of 500,000 copies by February 1977; three months prior to the film premiere. By the time *Star Wars* was released on May 25, 1977, eager fans were finding it challenging to acquire the novelization. But that was soon rectified, and by April 1978, the *nineteenth* printing of the film's story was released touting OVER FIVE MILLION COPIES in print. Since then, over 200 novels have been published under the *Star Wars* banner, with thousands of other books released (children's, young adult, behind the scenes, reference, story and activity books), expanding the *Star Wars* universe.

Thus began the first of three Ages (for now) of *Star Wars* literature. The Golden Age of *Star Wars* literature began with that first adaptation of what is now called *A New Hope*, and lasted a few years past the release of *Return of the Jedi*. Following this film, the demand for *Star Wars* diminished. Perhaps it's more accurate to say that the production of *Star Wars* related material diminished. Lacking any movie to create a tie-in to, most *Star Wars* merchandise petered out around 1986 — coinciding with the end of the *Droids* and *Ewoks* animated series'. But fans were still hungry for more tales from a galaxy far, far away. Sensing this, Lucasfilm commissioned author Timothy Zahn and publisher Bantam-Spectra to release a new book, the first in a proposed trilogy, in June 1991.

The Silver Age debuted with **Heir to the Empire**, which was greeted with fervorous sales and signaled that the interest in the Original Trilogy was still strong. A new line of books (and comics) paved the way into this new Age, and the eventual introduction of the newest film trilogy, The Prequels (1999-2005). As with the Original Trilogy, the books (transitioned back to Del Rey from 1999 onwards) supported the tales brought on by the films, introducing new Eras in the *Star Wars* Universe. Many adventures continued to occur around (or between) the films, but new tales were also being developed centuries prior to the films, as well as the exploration of "the future," where Luke, Leia, and Han

29

FROM THE FURTHER ADVENTURES OF
LUKE SKYWALKER, BASED ON THE CHARACTERS
AND SITUATIONS CREATED BY GEORGE LUCAS

SPLINTER
OF THE
MIND'S EYE

A new novel by
Alan Dean
Foster

continued their adventures after *Return of the Jedi*.

Since 1991, these adventures have never slowed down. They have only changed in status. The current publishing era, The Disney Era, is marked by the unprecedented sale of Lucasfilm to the Walt Disney Corporation in 2012. That signaled the moment when fans first heard the promise of a third series of films, The Sequel Trilogy, debuting in 2015. There were no plans to adapt the more popular existing novels, and any new stories would certainly conflict with the currently established canon. Therefore, The Disney Age began with its first edict, which was to label all previous works as *Legends* material, and promising that all literature (books, comics, short stories, video games, etc.) released from this point forward would be part of a new cohesive canon. These last few years of *Star Wars* literature have thereby been freed of the bindings of decades of weighty continuity, while also reaping the benefits of newer films and shows to draw additional stories from.

THE GOLDEN AGE

The novels that encompass The Golden Age of *Star Wars* literature laid the initial, and sparse, groundwork for the pantheon of titles to come. Originally published by Ballantine Books (which would soon transition to a new imprint — Del Rey), these ten adult fiction titles were only a mere fraction of the content published during this era, with children's books and comics making up the bulk. Yet the biggest contribution these titles offered was the beginnings of an attempt to form a cohesive universe of stories told by different writers. Certainly a first for an Intellectual Property of this magnitude. Three of the titles consisted of prose adaptations of the films in the Original Trilogy: **Star Wars: From the Adventures of Luke Skywalker** by George Lucas (1977; ghost-written by Alan Dean Foster), **The Empire Strikes Back** by Donald F. Glut (1980), and **Return of the Jedi** by James Khan (1983). Each book fleshed out the events of the film to a small degree, while creating a story that mirrored the events of the movie. Foster's book was not simply a one-to-one adaptation of the film. Based on Lucas' screenplay, the novel contains several deleted scenes including Luke Skywalker meeting his friends Camie and Fixer at Tosche Station, as well as Chewbacca receiving a medal at the award ceremony. (*And the prologue, which essentially serves as the opening crawl from the film, lays out the storyline for the prequels that would follow two decades later — ed.*) These additional elements would form the basis for what would be called the Expanded Universe (EU) over the next 35 years. **The Empire Strikes Back** adaptation also contained at least one deleted scene, in addition to other minor embellishments and differences from the movie, but **Return of the Jedi** appears to only have embellishments, and some apocryphal ones at that (such as Luke's uncle Owen Lars being identified as Obi-Wan's brother).

The second novel released was the very first book to expand the stories beyond the film. It debuted in February 1978, less than a year after the release of *A New Hope* and was part of George Lucas' shrewd plan to create a sequel to his film in the off-chance *Star Wars* was a flop. Alan Dean Foster was contracted for this book at the same time he was hired to write the film adaptation, and the story was optioned as a potential filmable low-budget sequel. Should *Star Wars* have tanked at the box office, **Splinter of the Minds' Eye** could have served as the basis for a television special, or even the continuation of stories in book form. It very obviously does not utilize Han Solo or Chewbacca (reportedly due to Harrison Ford not having signed up for any sequels), and is set on limited locations without major space battles.

As a further lead-in to *Empire*, Lucasfilm hired sci-fi author Brian Daley to write a trilogy of titles based on the adventures of Han Solo. He may not have been part of **Splinter of the Minds' Eye**, but he was a popular enough character to warrant his own titles. **Han Solo at Stars' End** and **Han Solo's Revenge** were both released in 1979, with **Han Solo and the Lost Legacy** arriving in early 1980. Unlike **Splinter of the Minds' Eye**, which took place between the first and second films (Episodes IV and V for the initiated), the Han Solo stories were set prior to his time with the Rebellion, and featured a number of new and intriguing characters and settings.

The final trilogy of adult fiction books released during The Golden Age focused on another popular character from the films, Lando Calrissian. As with the Han Solo titles, these stories explored Lando's adventures prior to owning Cloud City, as seen in *Empire*, and joining the Rebellion in *Jedi*. They vamped on a line of dialogue between Han and Lando in *The Empire Strikes Back* that indicated Lando had owned the *Millennium Falcon* prior to Han. **Lando Calrissian and the Mindharp of Sharu**, **Lando Calrissian and the Flamewind of Oseon**, and **Lando Calrissian and the Starcave of ThonBoka** were all written by L. Neil Smith and were published between July and November 1983.

THE SILVER AGE

This Era of the *Star Wars* literature timeline is the longest, covering just over 20 years. It is broken into mostly chronological eras following the events of *Return of the Jedi*, but also has titles that visit times prior to the Original Trilogy as well as during the events of the films.

THE NEW REPUBLIC ERA

In June of 1991, Bantam-Spectra published Timothy Zahn's **Heir to the Empire**, which was the first part of a trilogy set five years after the events of *Return of the Jedi*. This book became an immediate success, making its way to number one on the *New York Times* bestseller list, and helped to create the basis for the Expanded Universe. It introduced new characters to the pantheon including alien mastermind Grand Admiral Thrawn, former Palpatine assassin Mara Jade, smuggler Talon Karrde, and Bothan Senator Borsk Fey'lya. Knowing a good thing when they see it, Lucasfilm began planning for further adventures. The next wave of books debuted in January 1994 with **The Truce At Bakura** (Kathy Tyers) taking place immediately following the Battle of Endor (in *Return of the Jedi*). Soon a timeline was created to help readers and fans understand when a particular title took place. The

zero point of the timeline was identified as The Battle of Yavin, or the destruction of the first Death Star in *A New Hope*. This was year zero and the recent releases were identified as the number of years ABY (After the Battle of Yavin). A timeframe for The Original Trilogy was established, with *Empire* taking place 3 years after *A New Hope* and *Jedi* taking place one year after *Empire*. From there, different Eras were established to further categorize the titles with The Thrawn Trilogy and subsequent works occurring in the New Republic era, which was set 5-25 years ABY.

At this time a number of books were released that followed the three main characters (Luke, Leia & Han), such as the Kevin J. Anderson trilogy focusing on Luke building a new Jedi Academy, and **The Courtship of Princess Leia** which follows Han's struggle to woo the woman that would eventually become his wife. But some of the best titles of this time are the fan-favorite paperbacks by Michael A. Stackpole that explore a group of pilots known as Rogue Squadron. The series began with four titles to start with and continued with another batch in the late

90s. A new trilogy based on the adventures of Han Solo was also created during this time by veteran sci-fi writer A.C. Crispin. The Han Solo Trilogy followed his time as a young man, and through his initial meetings with the Hutts and eventually Lando Calrissian, and even interwove itself with the events of Daley's Solo Trilogy and Smith's Calrissian Trilogy.

During this time Lucasfilm also created a multimedia project and began heavily promoting it, calling it everything but a movie. In addition to a novel, **Shadows of the Empire** (Steve Perry, 1996), it was also comprised of a comic mini-series, a soundtrack, a video game and action figures (which had only returned to production the year before), and sought to tell a complete story about how the Rebels attempted to rescue Han Solo from Boba Fett between *Empire* and *Jedi*. A second wave of X-Wing titles were published, this time by author Aaron Allston. **Wraith Squadron**, **Iron Fist**, and **Solo Command** were released between 1998-99, with Michael Stackpole returning for **Isard's Revenge** (1999) and Allston's conclusion to the series (for now), **Starfighters of Adumar** (1999). Fan-favorite Corran Horn also returned in his own title, and the first first-person *Star Wars* book was released: **I, Jedi** (Michael Stackpole, 1998).

THE PREQUEL ERA

Lucas returned to the helm of director in 1999 and released Episode I: *The Phantom Menace*, which took place some 32 years BBY (Before the Battle of Yavin). This signified the second major publishing wave of The Silver Age. The publishing rights had returned to Del Rey books, which separated their timeline into two major areas: The Prequel Era (also called the Rise of the Empire era, and spanning 1,000 to 0 BBY) and the New Jedi Order era which took place after the New Republic Era, and covered 25 to 37 ABY.

The continuity of the Expanded Universe took the franchise to new heights. In 1999, Del Rey introduced an ambitious project of their own — The New Jedi Order series. The plan of this arc of books was to release a massive interrelated story that spanned five hardcovers over five years. These "core" books would be supplemented with a series of paperback releases in between, telling smaller stories that spun out of the events in the hardcovers. At this time in the New Republic Era, the galaxy is invaded by a new, force-immune species known as the Yuuzhan Vong. Luke and his fledgling Jedi Order and Leia and her New Republic are not ready for the barbarism that comes with this new threat, and must make sacrifices. The first and most polarizing sacrifice — one that made headlines in newspapers like *USA Today* — was the death of Chewbacca (**Vector Prime**; R.A. Salvatore, 1999). Del Rey needed a "hook" to show the dangers of this new era, and what better way than killing "the family dog," so to speak. Many fans were not happy with this development, but that was the way publishing went as it moved forward in time. Chewie was dead and no stories that occurred after 25 ABY would feature his shaggy visage.

All in all, nineteen titles (plus three eBooks), made up the bulk of the New Jedi Order series, centered on five hardcovers included the aforementioned **Vector Prime**, plus **Balance Point** (Kathy Tyers, 2000), **Star By Star** (Troy Denning, 2001), **Destiny's Way** (Walter Jon Williams, 2002), and **The Unifying Force** (James Luceno, 2003).

The stories in this era also benefited from the expanding *Star Wars* universe produced in the prequel films. Though there was nothing overtly mentioned about these new films, new ideals of the Force, planets, aliens, and other creatures made their way into the stories.

As with The Original Trilogy, novelizations of the new films were created in support of each release. **The Phantom Menace** (Terry Brooks, 1999), **Attack of the Clones** (R.A. Salvatore, 2002) and **Revenge of the Sith** (Matthew Stover, 2005) all expanded on the plots of the films, incorporating more scenes, deleted moments, or other author-invented elements to not only adapt the movie, but tie elements into the larger Expanded Universe. Episode I was the only film not to feature a prequel novel prior to

release, presumably due to the secrecy surrounding the storyline. However, it did receive a Qui-Gon/Obi-Wan prequel the following year providing a little more backstory about those characters (**Rogue Planet**; Greg Bear, 2000). **Darth Maul – Saboteur** (James Luceno, eBook) and **Darth Maul – Shadow Hunter** (Michael Reaves, Hardcover) dove into the master and apprentice relationship between Darth Sidious and Maul. Additionally, **Cloak of Deception** (James Luceno, 2001) provided a fascinating look at the intricacies of the Trade Federation and the machinations Darth Sidious used to sway the galaxy to his plans, revealing he was truly a phantom menace.

The Approaching Storm (Alan Dean Foster, 2002), a prequel to Episode II, told the story behind an Obi-Wan line in *Attack of the Clones* where he stated that he and Anakin just returned from a border dispute on Ansion. Following that, and the release of Episode II, the majority of titles that were released told the tales of The Clone Wars, which was originally teased as a battle in *A New Hope*. Fans were now able to experience the three years' worth of battles between the Republic and the Separatists. The Clone Wars concluded with several titles centered around the final film in the Prequel Trilogy, *Revenge of the Sith*, and the rise of Darth Vader.

THE LEGACY ERA

By 2006, Del Rey and Lucasfilm had entered their third major era of the modern publishing program. The Legacy Era, which encompassed anything beyond 37 years ABY, continued the ongoing saga of the Skywalker Family started within the New Republic and New Jedi Order eras. Similar to the sprawling New Jedi Order series, the Legacy of the Force storyline was told across multiple titles. But this time it was simpler; only nine books, with three core Hardcovers. It featured three authors round-robining through the titles: Aaron Allston, Karen Traviss, and Troy Denning. The era ended with **X-Wing: Mercy Kill** (Aaron Allston, 2012), the first hardcover X-Wing title and Allston's final book before his death. While the main storyline extended after *Return of the Jedi*, there was still much work being created in the other publishing eras. As such, it was also a time for growth and experimentation with the stories as new writers were brought into the fold to try their hand at writing a *Star Wars* novel. Since the Prequels had been completed, and as far as anyone knew were the last *Star Wars* films to be made, Lucasfilm allowed for stories to pop up in both the Old Republic era (25,000-1000 BBY) and Before the Republic (37,000-25,000 BBY). Among the titles were stories that dealt with a Sith Lord mentioned in the Prequels, Darth Bane, whose Rule of Two was the basis for the modern Sith Order.

One of the more experimental titles was the 2009 book **Death Troopers** (Joe Schreiber) and its prequel, **Red Harvest** (Joe Schreiber, 2010). One of the few areas that *Star Wars* had not previously ventured into was horror, and Schreiber filled this niche nicely. These books found a fan base, and Schreiber was asked to write one further title that had its share of gothic elements: **Darth Maul: Lockdown** (2014).

With the completion of the Prequel

films, there was now the ability to set books between two trilogies, including the *Coruscant Nights* Trilogy (**Jedi Twilight**, **Street of Shadows**, **Patterns of Force**; Michael Reaves, 2008-2009) and the follow-up book, coincidentally titled **The Last Jedi** (Michael Reaves & Maya Kaathryn Bohnhoff, 2013). But two of the titles that many people talk most about include a tale of Obi-Wan Kenobi and his relocation to Tatooine after the events of *Revenge of the Sith* — simply titled **Kenobi** (John Jackson Miller, 2013) — and the history of Palpatine and his Sith master, **Darth Plagueis** (James Luceno, 2012).

The end of this publishing era featured a series of Classic Era stories revealing unknown points in the lives of the main characters, as well as creating some one-off titles from these massive adventures, just to allow fans a break from the ongoing sagas. Timothy Zahn crafted a loose trilogy featuring Mara Jade and the Rebellion heroes, culminating with an *Ocean's Eleven* style heist story with Han, Lando and a crew of thieves. The final two books published were a duology bundled under

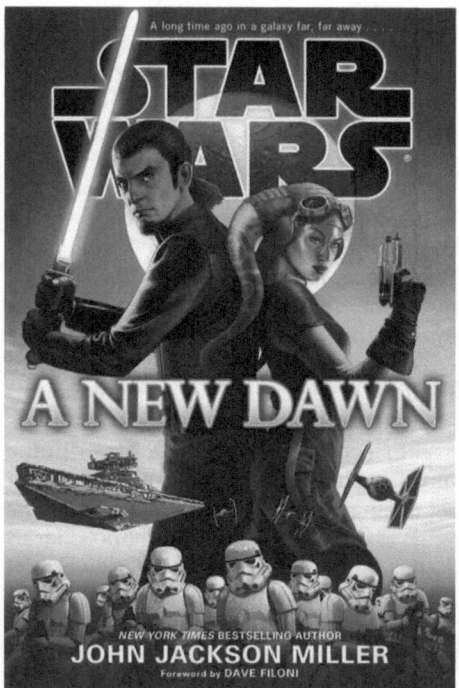

the banner of *Empire and Rebellion*, with the third title being repurposed for the new Canon of the most recent publishing era.

THE DISNEY AGE

The world of *Star Wars* changed once again rather unexpectedly on October 26, 2012, when it was announced that The Walt Disney Company had purchased Lucasfilm from George Lucas, and that a new trilogy of films, The Sequel Trilogy, was being planned. Lucasfilm announced about a year and a half later that in order to better serve the making of the sequels, all prior literature produced was considered apocryphal. Only the films and the recent television series, starting with *The Clone Wars* and including the forthcoming *Rebels*, would be part of the new canon. Any new book, comic, video game, short story or series would become part of the new canon, while all previous work was labeled as *Legends*. This caused some consternation in the fan community, where many constant readers felt that the "effort" they had put into reading all of the stories in the previous 35 years were for naught. In reality, the only portion of the previous timeline that was completely

wiped out and ignored are the events following *Return of The Jedi*. Some stories and characters were re-canonized in new ways, while other stories can still exist in the new canon, until they are specifically contradicted. Either way, the previous books still exist and most are still in print. Because there's no reason to *not* enjoy a fun story for the sake of continuity in this fictitious universe.

And so, in September 2014, John Jackson Miller's **A New Dawn**, an aptly named tale serving as a prequel to the TV series *Rebels*, hit shelves. Other Classic Era titles included a new Luke Skywalker story, **Heir to the Jedi** (Kevin Hearn, 2015), which was actually meant to be part of the previous *Empire and Rebellion* series, **Tarkin** (James Luceno, 2014) and the video game tie-ins **Battlefront: Twilight Company** and **Battlefront II: Inferno Squad** (Alexander Freed, 2015-17). Only after a few books were released, and more information about the timeframe of the next film was announced, were authors allowed to start prowling the timeline post-Episode VI. Chuck Wendig's *Aftermath* trilogy took place only 4-5 years ABY (so, immediately following the events of *Return of the Jedi*), and served as a lead-in to events that would eventually feature in *The Force Awakens*, including the Battle of Jakku.

In December of 2015 the seventh *Star Wars* film, *The Force Awakens*, was released. Unlike the previous films, where the novel was released hand-in-hand with the film, Alan Dean Foster's novelization wasn't released until one month later, most likely due to the secrecy of the plot of the film. Four tie-in short eBooks were collected in print in **Tales from a Galaxy Far, Far Away Volume 1: Aliens** (Landry Q. Walker, 2016), and soon, the publishing efforts were fully supporting the new films, which were slated for one movie per year. An ambitious schedule!

Bloodline (Claudia Gray, 2016) was the next hardcover novel released and told a political tale with Leia Organa in the years preceding *The Force Awakens*. Other titles included a tie-in for *Rogue One: A Star Wars Story*, called **Catalyst: A Rogue One Story** (James Luceno, 2016), and a

Han Solo and Lando Calrissian adventure called **Last Shot** (Daniel José Older, 2018) which was tied in with the release of **Solo: A Star Wars Story Expanded Edition** (Mur Lafferty, 2018), the standalone *Star Wars* film that year. The following year saw Timothy Zahn re-adapt and flesh out his short story "Mist Encounter" (about Thrawn's first meeting with the Empire) as part of the new canon in **Thrawn** (2017), which was the first of six books (and two trilogies, so far) about this amazing strategist and tactician. At this time the character was also included in the *Star Wars Rebels* television series, increasing his appeal with fans everywhere. Del Rey also released prequel stories on the origin of fan favorite **Phasma** (Delilah S. Dawson, 2017), and an Episode VIII prequel focusing on the gambling planet **Canto Bight** (Saladin Ahmed, Rae Carson, Mira Grant & John Jackson Miller, 2017).

As with *The Force Awakens*, the adaption for *The Last Jedi*, subtitled **The Expanded Edition** (Jason Fry, 2018) was released approximately three months after the film.

By 2019, tie-ins were not just for movies as **Galaxy's Edge: Black Spire** (Delilah S. Dawson, 2019) created a backstory for the newly opened land in the Disney theme parks, also called Galaxy's Edge. Other titles delved further into different Eras.

The final story created before the release of the culmination of the The Sequel Trilogy was Rebecca Roanhorse's **Resistance Reborn** (2019). This title set up some additional backstory that led into the release of *The Rise of Skywalker* which was again adapted in an **Expanded Edition** (Rae Carson, 2020) several months later. 2020 celebrated the biggest *Star Wars* event since The New Jedi Order, with the unveiling of a massive multi-author project set during The High Republic (circa 300-82 years BBY). It featured five authors (Charles Soule, Cavan Scott, Claudia Gray, Daniel José Older and Justina Ireland) taking turns writing new adult fiction, young adult stories, middle-grade books and elementary storybooks that highlighted the golden age of the Jedi and their trials and tribulations. These High Republic stories returned to the large-scale continuities of The Silver Age, like The New Jedi Order.

Many other tales are planned to continue exploring the history of the *Star Wars* universe, from hundreds of years in the past, to tales well into the Sequel Trilogy.

The following are some of the highlights of the last 45 years of *Star Wars* literature.

SPLINTER OF THE MINDS' EYE
BY ALAN DEAN FOSTER

The first original *Star Wars* spin-off has Luke and Leia, with the droids, crashing on the planet Mimban where Luke learns of the Kaiburr crystal (re-introduced in the Disney Era as a kyber crystal, the power source of Jedi lightsabers), which can magnify his Force powers. The rebels team up with a local woman, Halla, and a pair of creatures, Hee and Kee, in order to find the crystal before the Empire, led by Captain-Supervisor Grammel. Darth Vader arrives to search for the crystal as well, and he and Luke have a lightsaber fight, during which Luke cuts off the arm of the Sith Lord before forcing him into a pit. The heroes then escape to continue their adventures. To readers of the era, this was a perfectly plausible sequel to *Star Wars*, except that by the time *The Empire Strikes Back* came out (or *The Star Wars Holiday Special* before that), there was no mention of these events.

HEIR TO THE EMPIRE
BY TIMOTHY ZAHN

Zahn set his novel in a post-*Return of the Jedi* world, which at the time provided a clear and open slate in which to craft new adventures. He chose to feature the characters of Luke, Leia & Han (now married), Chewbacca, the droids R2-D2 & C-3PO, plus several other classic characters such as Lando, Mon Mothma, and Admiral Ackbar. Knowing that the Emperor was dead, and that the Rebellion would have to learn how to govern themselves, he crafted a number of new characters to serve as allies and enemies in this new era. Grand Admiral Thrawn was the new and tactically superior foe that the New Republic would face. He was joined by smuggler Talon Karrde, ex-Imperial spy Mara Jade, and the mad Jedi clone Joruus C'baoth. The three books that comprise the trilogy, which also included **Dark Force Rising** (1992) and **The Last Command** (1993), would take the characters to new worlds (including the galactic capitol of Coruscant; the Prequel films would retain the name which originated in this series), introduce new technology and ships, and new alien species. The trilogy also included the birth of Han and Leia's force sensitive twins, Jaina and Jacen, which would become major characters in the stories as the Era continued.

X-WING: ROGUE SQUADRON
BY MICHAEL A. STACKPOLE

The first book in this series, simply titled **X-Wing: Rogue Squadron** (1996), follows Wedge Antilles (a minor pilot seen in all three Original Trilogy films) as he assembles a new version of this squadron. The pilots are a mix of humans and aliens, including a mentioned-but-never-seen-on-film Bothan, a Twi'lek, a Shistavanen, and a Rodian. Rogue Nine, Corran Horn, was a particular standout character that

proved to be popular with fans and would eventually get an expanded arc through numerous books, as he discovered latent Jedi talent. These X-Wing books also introduced a handful of new Imperial characters to challenge the Rogues, including Ysanne Isard and Kirtan Loor, both members of the Imperial Intelligence community. Stackpole would write three more X-Wing titles, including **Wedge's Gamble**, **The Krytos Trap** and **The Bacta War** between 1996 and 97.

DEATH TROOPERS
BY JOE SCHREIBER

The story involves the outbreak of a plague on a derelict prison ship that turns the crew into zombies. Fans were also pleasantly surprised when a certain Corellian smuggler and his wookiee companion became trapped on the vessel, raising the stakes for this decidedly creepy title. It came off as a mix of *Star Wars*, *Alien*, and *Dawn of the Dead*. The follow-up was set thousands of years prior, and explained the origins of the virus that caused the outbreak.

by General Grievous; immediately before the opening moments of Episode III. Elements of the story were paraphrased in the opening crawl. The novelization of **Revenge of the Sith** (Matthew Stover, 2005) does much the same thing that the other adaptations had done, with fleshing out moments in the film, and for the most part, just presenting the story as seen on screen. This was followed by **Dark Lord** (James Luceno, 2005) and showed the immediate aftermath of the succession of Emperor Palpatine and the rise of the Empire. It also served the story of Anakin's first days as Darth Vader, and his understanding of what his life has become. It was one of the first books to actually humanize Vader and along with the other two titles, make a fantastic trilogy.

DARTH BANE: PATH OF DESTRUCTION
BY DREW KARPYSHYN

Path of Destruction (2006), **Rule of Two** (2007), and **Dynasty of Evil** (2009), all written by Drew Karpyshyn, tell the rise and fall of this Sith legend. Set 1,000 years before *A New Hope*, **Path of Destruction** merged elements from the successful comic series *Tales of the Jedi* (where the Sith were not just an antithesis to the Jedi, but originally a race of beings interested in the Dark Side) plus the Sith lore touched on in The Prequels. It begins with a young miner who joins the ranks of the Sith Army. His growth in the Dark Side allows him to eventually become Darth Bane, a powerful Sith Lord that would alter the nature of the Sith in the galaxy forever

KENOBI
BY JOHN JACKSON MILLER

This 2013 book picks up with the Jedi, now calling himself "Ben," settling on the desert world Tatooine in order to keep watch over young Luke Skywalker. It features encounters with Tusken Raiders and various settlers, as the former Jedi tries not to draw too much attention to himself. Much of the upcoming preview footage for the Disney+ show, also called *Kenobi*, appears to draw elements from Miller's book, including Ben riding on an eopie, who in the book is named Rooh.

THE DARK LORD TRILOGY
BY JAMES LUCENO & MATTHEW STOVER

The end of The Clone Wars, and the immediate precursor to Episode III is a story that depicts Anakin and Obi-Wan trying to protect Chancellor Palpatine. **Labyrinth of Evil** (James Luceno, 2005) picks up towards the end of the War where Obi-Wan and Anakin are tasked with capturing Separatist leader Nute Gunray. The story ends with a battle on Coruscant and the abduction of Chancellor Palpatine

DARTH PLAGUEIS
BY JAMES LUCENO

One of the more popular titles of the pre-Disney Era is **Darth Plagueis** by James Luceno (2012). Named after the Sith master of Darth Sidious (first mentioned in *Revenge of the Sith*), it tells the story of Palpatine's rise to power. While the book initially seemed to focus on this other Sith Lord, it makes great use of a split narrative to show Plagueis with his master, and then how Palpatine became indoctrinated as Sidious, learning his own Dark Side secrets from his master. It also weaves its narrative in between the moments of other titles, specifically some of The Clone Wars novels, showing the moments behind the moments, in almost a *Rosencrantz and Guildenstern* fashion.

BLOODLINE
BY CLAUDIA GRAY

Set almost three decades after the Battle of Yavin, this political thriller features Leia Organa, now a respected Senator in the New Republic. She navigates political and Imperial treachery while news that she is also the daughter of one of the most ruthless villains the galaxy has ever known, Darth Vader. The book sows an interesting mystery and also introduces the beginnings of The Resistance seen in the Sequel Trilogy.

FROM A CERTAIN POINT OF VIEW
VARIOUS

This is a special anthology created for the 40th Anniversary of *A New Hope* in 2017. It features 40 stories by 40 authors that range from comical to adventurous. Each author was allowed to pick an element from the original film to expand on, similar to what the **Tales From The Mos Eisley Cantina** anthology had done. But authors were not limited to the one location, and the tales are arranged in chronological order, from the Empire capturing Leia's ship, through the adventures on Tatooine, and the destruction of the original Death Star. The book was such a hit with fans that a second volume, with 40 stories surrounding *The Empire Strikes Back*, was released in 2020.

LIGHT OF THE JEDI
BY CHARLES SOULE

Kicking off The High Republic collection of tales is this novel by Charles Soule, already a fan favorite for his *Poe Dameron* and *Darth Vader* comic series. The story starts approximately 300 years BBY as the High Republic open a new space station called Starlight Beacon. New characters, mostly Jedi, must come together to aide various worlds as a catastrophe in hyperspace rains destruction on many worlds. But that is just

the beginning of the problems that the Jedi and the High Republic will face, as a new threat called The Nihil rise to challenge the supremacy of both.

Star Wars literature has something for everyone. It continues, and supports, the stories of the familiar characters from the films (and television series) for those that want to know more about Darth Vader, Luke Skywalker, and even the lesser-known characters on the screen. It also creates new worlds, events, and characters that engage in the same universe of science-fiction and fantasy elements. There are tales of horror, lighthearted adventures, and technical military fiction to enthrall and capture the imaginations of all types of readers. Most importantly, however, the continued stories produced under the *Star Wars* banner are invitations for people to read. They entice individuals, especially younger readers, to pick up a book and spend some time with friends. Friends who just happen to be from a galaxy far, far away.

• • •

CONVERSATIONS
WITH THE
FATHER

A Memoir about Richard Matheson, My Dad and God

CHRIS MATHESON

Chris and Richard Matheson on the set of *The Night Strangler* (1973)

A CONVERSATION WITH THE SON
Chris Matheson — the *bare•*bones interview
by John Scoleri

Born in 1959, Chris Matheson is the youngest child of Richard Matheson, author of **I Am Legend**, **The Shrinking Man**, and countless others (not that he needs an introduction to our readers). A successful comedic writer (he's the co-creator of the characters "Bill & Ted" with Ed Solomon), Chris has written a fascinating memoir, **Conversations with the Father**, which details his relationship with his father, and how his father's spiritual beliefs ultimately led to their estrangement. Presented in the form of a flip-book (like a classic double novel of years past), the book also contains a humorous story (also titled **Conversations with the Father**, as written by 'Gordon Whitehead'). It's the tale of one man's interactions with God, inspired by Chris' father's metaphysical work, **The Path**. I had the pleasure of speaking with Chris about his new memoir and his father shortly before the release of his book.

bare•bones: I want to start with the title: **Conversations with the Father: A Memoir about Richard Matheson, My Dad and God.** *I'll be perfectly honest. When I sat down to read the book, I was prepared for you to take the position of, 'here's how my father and my spiritual beliefs differed, and why his were wrong and mine were right.' And that isn't the thrust of the book at all. So to that end, I'm curious about the inclusion of God in the subtitle. God is noticeably absent from the memoir half of the book.*

CHRIS MATHESON: One of the factors was the double quality of the thing; that it's two books in one, and the second part — the Gordon Whitehead part — is *all* about God. In terms of the part about my Dad, I think it's fair to say that he was a God-like figure for me. I mean, he was, for sure. I really idolized him — I thought he was the greatest, and I couldn't have looked up to him more. It's funny, his belief system doesn't really have God in it, and that always kind of baffled me. It's like, there's no God here. I remember saying to him sometimes, "Who did all this? Who built this crazy elaborate system?" Well, it was us; eventually it turns out it was humans, somehow, in a way that I never really understood. I always thought that God was implicit in it, like there had to be some architect behind all this stuff that he was positing.

BB: You start the book explaining that you were not close with your mother or older siblings growing up, but as a boy you idolized your father. And it seems like it was all in the normal father/ son ways. When did you become aware of your father's work as a writer, and a somewhat famous one at that? Did that impact your admiration for him?

MATHESON: I was aware of it at a pretty young age. I *so* loved my Dad, and wanted to know everything about him. I knew he was something, when I was a kid, because I remember going on to movie sets, and just being aware that he didn't just have your average job. I started reading his stuff probably when I was ten or eleven. I remember reading **Hell House** when it came out, which was a pretty fucking intense book for a twelve year-old kid to read. It was pretty hairy, you know? I remember reading that when I was twelve. I had read all the **Shock** books; all the short story collections. I remember sitting in the living room, and pulling out these leather-bound copies that he had, and I would just sort of burn through them. So I had read all the short stories by the time I was probably eleven, and then I got to the novels a bit later. **Hell House** might very well have been the first one I read, which is pretty funny.

BB: *That's an intense one to begin with . . .*

MATHESON: That's a *really* intense one.

BB: *Your father was part of a group of writers who were closely connected, including Charles Beaumont, William F. Nolan, George Clayton Johnson, and others. I assume these folks were around as you were growing up. Were you aware of who they were?*

MATHESON: There was socializing that took place. He was pretty close with Chuck Beaumont. They were peers, and they sort of competed in a friendly way, I think. And they were friends. Chuck died so young, in 1967. I was just a kid when Chuck died. Bill Nolan was around at times. I have no memories of George Clayton Johnson; I know that he was around, like Jerry Sohl, and maybe Bob Bloch sometimes. He did socialize, but my Dad didn't really like socializing very much. He was really a *writerly* kind of writer; in a big way, a very introspective, quiet guy, who liked to be alone in his office and just write for eight hours a day. I mean there was that other part of him; he and my Mom did do a lot of socializing. They had a lot of friends. I always felt my Mom kinda dragged him into that, and he went along with it.

BB: *I wanted to ask you about Chuck Beaumont, in particular. Your families were very similar — Chuck and Helen close in age to your parents, with four kids in the same age ranges as you and your siblings. Suddenly, Chuck dies, followed by his wife Helen just a few years later. Did those deaths impact you, given those similarities?*

MATHESON: Not in the way of, *holy shit* — *that could happen to us*. I didn't have those thoughts. But my parents were close enough with Chuck and Helen Beaumont that after they both died, their kids, especially the two younger ones, Elizabeth and Greg, would come and stay at our house for weekends, or during the summer they'd stay for maybe a week. We spent a lot of time with the Beaumont kids after their parents died.

BB: *Both your older brother RC and sister Ali are writers, and you became a writer as well. Not to assume your father's spiritual beliefs, but did that seem to be predestined?*

MATHESON: Well, apples and trees, you know. I didn't want to be a writer, for a pretty long time, because I didn't want to compete with my Dad. I thought he was sort of this towering figure — which he was. I thought, well shit, I've got to find my own path. I did some other stuff. I thought I wanted to be an actor for a while, which was very misguided. And then I wanted to direct for a while, and I devoted quite a lot of energy into being a play director, and then trying to be a film director. With very, very limited success, I would say. It was only as years went by that I thought, well, this writing thing comes pretty naturally, and once I started writing comedy specifically, I felt more comfortable with that. My Dad did write comedy sometimes, but he wasn't really a *comedy* writer at all, so it was a different enough thing. You know, lawyer's kids a lot of times become lawyers, and athlete's kids become athletes, and scientist's kids become scientists. You just grow up with it, and you know it. I would say we all probably understood the writing life pretty well, because we saw it. It wasn't very mysterious to us. We kinda grasped it, and that's helpful in some ways.

BB: I will say that what stands out is that you've all been successful at it.

MATHESON: I don't really know, and it's not really my place to speak for my siblings, *at all*, but I don't think writing was Ali's first choice. I think like me, she came to it a little bit later. I think it was Richard's first choice — I think that's what he wanted to do from a pretty early age. But I think like me, Ali sort of drifted into it.

*BB: You mention how in the mid-1970s, your father changed, having read a book (**Thinking & Destiny** by Harold Percival). It seems like this fell somewhere around the writing of **Bid Time Return**, and certainly before the writing of **What Dreams May Come**. Did you have a sense of his spiritual beliefs before that time?*

MATHESON: As I mention in the book, I kind of grew up steeped in metaphysical thinking. All these realities that are absolute certainties, pertaining to life after death, and teleportation, and telekinesis, and ESP. I knew all that. That was just part of our reality. I alluded to *Fate* magazine, which was *always* around. He read them, and he liked it. It was just life. I don't know that *he* changed. He *might* have; I can't really say. I know *I* did. I started looking at things differently, because I was just getting older, and I'm naturally a very skeptical person. *Very* skeptical. I don't take things at face value. I don't just buy things — I just *don't*. I'm more like my Mom that way, because my Mom was also like that. In a family of believers, I was a big non-believer, but I would say that she didn't really believe, either. She was a little more agnostic, let's say, and I'm the atheist in our family. Strongly the atheist in the family. She was kind of agnostic and didn't really buy stuff, either, but she was trying to keep the peace, I guess. She would go around it, and I would not. And as I got older, I developed an irascible personality

in some ways, and I just started looking at it differently. In terms of my Dad, if I was to speculate, he was getting older, and he was terrified of death. *Terrified* of death. **Terrified** of death. Now, nobody looks forward to death, I don't think, unless they're in excruciating pain and it's relief, but he was really, *really* scared of death, and I think as he got older, it got to be more of a thing. Now that's speculation — I don't *know* that — but it makes sense to me.

*BB: Based on Percival (and your father's) beliefs on how that which we do in life will manifest itself in our future lives, do you think the Richard Matheson who became a proponent of Harold Percival would ever have written novels like **I Am Legend**, **Hell House** or some of his most famous short stories? I've read interviews later in his life where he downplayed the works he had written that are widely considered horror (I believe he preferred to refer to them as terror tales), and it would seem that in some part that may have been due to his evolving beliefs about putting such material out into the world.*

MATHESON: I don't think he would have. I think he was on the record of saying he wouldn't have. He would kind of denigrate those things, *well, I don't want to do that.* Sort of like he transcended it, or something, which I thought was a mistaken way of looking at it. And he didn't want to be scared, you know? My Dad was a really *scared* guy. He was a *really scared* guy. A very frightened guy, and look, I kinda get it. He didn't have a Dad, and he grows up in the Depression, and they're poor, and he's sent into the fucking front in World War II at eighteen years old, and has machine-gun bullets whizzing over his head, and he's steeped in all this bizarre Christian Science beliefs . . . He was a very, very, very scared guy. And I think he didn't want to stay there. To me, he was looking for scaffolding to escape it. And for me, the big book, I mean *the* one, if I've got to pick one and go, well there's Dad — it's **The Shrinking Man**. Cause **The Shrinking Man** just nails it. **The Shrinking Man** is everything. It's him. And he knows what's happening to him. He knows. He writes it very poetically. It's a beautiful book, I think. And then at the end, he metaphysicalizes it, if that's the right word. I *like* the ending — I'm not criticizing the ending, but the metaphysics come in, and that's the start, and they never go away after that.

So something like **I Am Legend**, no, I don't think he would have written it, because it's raw. It's naked. It's kind of stark and horrible and brutal — but really beautiful. To me, he never wrote anything more beautiful than the dog scene. I think that's just gorgeous. Gorgeous, and tremendously sad. Powerful, and dramatic.

I think what comes later, I don't think he wants to deal — I mean **Hell House** is the end, in terms of dealing with his fears in a raw way. There is nothing like that ever again. I mean, you could look at something like **Hunted Past Reason** — yeah, he's getting in to some intense shit, for sure — but he doesn't want to do it anymore. They get loftier around **Bid Time Return** and **What Dreams May Come**. And then, honestly, I don't know if there's another serious book after **What Dreams May Come**. I don't personally think there is — I think that's the last one. From my standpoint, that's the last one that counts. He doesn't want to be scared any more. And he doesn't want to be scared of death. He's willing to be scared in his early stuff, and that's why it's so great.

*BB: Several chapters in, your memoir truly becomes a conversation with your father, primarily over Percival's **Thinking & Destiny** and the beliefs your father took from that work. As those sections read like a transcript, I'm curious if those are based on particularly vivid memories of specific discussion you had with your Dad, or if it's more of an artistic license to communicate those discussions?*

MATHESON: Those are conversations we had, again and again and again. They're not tape recordings; they are based on my recollection. I probably made both of us a little more eloquent at times than maybe we were. But those are real conversations — they're real back-and-forths that we had on a number of occasions.

BB: Your father clearly had strong convictions when it came to Percival, and that comes across in your conversations. Often when your father would talk about adaptations of his work, he would point out that things would have been more successful had they just followed his script or story. While that's certainly the prerogative of an author, I couldn't help but hear his voice as I read those conversations in the book, and that same conviction that there was a single right answer — and it was his.

MATHESON: Yeah, and you can imagine that it was at times difficult to be that guy's son. Because you're right — *he knew*. He knew with absolute certainty. You know my Dad's work pretty damn well, so maybe you've even heard the CD, *Reality*. That's him. My wife listened to it with me, long, long ago, and she's like, wow, it's like he's scolding us. *This is absolute reality, and if you don't agree with me, what is wrong with you?* That was often his move, and I didn't like that. I didn't like that at all. That made me mad, and that was a big part of what went south. It was like, "Well, what's wrong with *you*? You *do* need to believe this stuff. Stop trying to pin it on *me*!"

BB: I can certainly see how someone with a natural inclination to be skeptical wanting to have the discussion. If the discussion ends at, "well, you just don't get it . . . "

MATHESON: Yeah. You are incapable of grasping it. It's too rarefied, somehow, for you. And *maybe* you'll evolve in a way that you will get it. It's like, *Oh come on — I can see right through you! I **know** you. Nobody knows you like your children, right? Nobody.* Especially a child who studies you. And I *studied* him. It's like, *Oh come on, Dad — you're just **scared**. Why can't you admit that? Why can't you just admit you're scared, instead of pulling this ridiculous move.* And then any criticism is just because other people can't grasp the magnificence of these ludicrous ideas that Percival is putting forth. Have you read **Thinking and Destiny**?

BB: No.

MATHESON: Well don't. It's terrible.

*BB: I have read **The Path** . . .*

MATHESON: **The Path** is my Dad's *popularization* of it, in a way, so a lot of the ideas are in there. Percival is utterly insufferable. I mean, why my Dad liked *that* book — god knows. Why he chose *that* one, out of all the books in the world . . . This guy, you just want to slap him. Oh my god, you are so monumentally brimming over with bullshit, Harold Percival.

*BB: Around 2000, following the publication of **The Path**, you wrote a story, "Mondays with the Lord," essentially poking fun at your Dad's book. That story, re-titled **Conversations with the Father**, and credited to 'Gordon Whitehead,' is presented alongside your memoir, in a classic 'double' format (where readers flip the book over to read the second title). You say that when you showed the story to your father, rather than triggering an argument, he found humor in it, and ended up contributing ideas to it. You also mention how humor was always one of your father's strengths, and I'm curious if you think he saw what you were doing with the piece, and chose to not let it bother him, or if he just saw it as a humorous piece and didn't see it as a commentary on his own beliefs?*

MATHESON: He knew that I was making fun of his beliefs. He commented on it specifically. There are very specific things that he believed in that I'm kind of mocking in the book, and he knew that. Of course he knew that. We had so many arguments by that point that he knew what I thought. I'm sure there was a part of him that was offended and annoyed, and irked — all that. But there was another part of him — well, there were several parts to this guy; he was a complicated man. He was a large man, in a lot of ways. There was a part of him that was just a supportive father. So there's that. There the professional writer; and the professional writer part of him is strong. It's always strong. It's like he can overcome whatever emotional complexity there might be, and he can just deal with something as a piece of work, because he's very, very strong that way. And then, the part that *I* like the most, that I like to think about the most, is

that he had this relationship with comedy. And I don't think people really realize how much comedy meant to my Dad. And how much he loved it. *Loved* it. **Loved** it. I mean he *adored* comedy. And he had really good taste in comedy. And he gravitated to it — and he took us to see it. In the bar room of my parent's house, there were framed black and white lithographs of Laurel and Hardy, Buster Keaton, Charlie Chaplin, Harold Lloyd and Harry Langdon, I think. Which just gives you an idea what comedy meant to this guy.

How funny the thing is? I don't know. I mean, I wrote it; how do I know. But he thought it was funny, and he responded to it on that level. And I love that, you know? I love that there was that part of him, that *loved* humor, and he *loved* playing, and he *loved* silliness. I point it out in the book, but I was really struck when I was re-reading **Hell House** recently, that the ending — I had forgotten the ending — that it just comes down to '*laugh at him*.' That's it! *That's* the answer! That's all there is. Laugh at Belasco, and you will strip him of his power. And it works. All you have to do is laugh at him. The power of laughter. He got it. He *knew* it. In his last venture into the dark, deep, heavy, scary, sexual place — cause it is — he ends it with the power of laughter. And that's part of my Dad. I like to think that's a part of it, too. It's incredible. It would be as if in "Duel," that the guy, David Mann, just pulls over his car and just stands there, laughing at the truck driver, and that's it — the truck driver just drives off a cliff. Like that's it. It absolutely undoes Belasco. What a beautiful, totally surprising ending. Because my Dad wrote horror — well, horror, science-fiction and fantasy. I don't personally think he's a very *funny* writer — I don't think that was his gift. I don't personally find any of his comedy any good; that's just me. I'm a comedy-guy, so I'm sort of snobby about comedy, but I don't think that's his great gift at all. But — fuck, man — he *loved* it. He *loved* it. And this guy's laugh was fantastic. I mean, when this guy roared with laughter, he just bellowed with laughter; totally uninhibited. His whole body would shake. He would laugh so hard he would cry. He would just laugh — and he laughed a lot. And he could be pretty funny, too.

*BB: The tone of the second half of the book — Gordon Whitehead's **Conversations with the Father** — is **very** different than that of the first half (the memoir). There were several moments, such as when 'The Father' describes the unfortunate circumstances under which some people have returned from the dead, that had me laughing out loud. I was reminded that, oh yeah, **this** is the guy who co-wrote the hilarious **Bill & Ted** movies. What do you hope readers take from the story?*

MATHESON: I hope they think it's funny. It's comedy, and I'm a comedy writer. I wanted it to be funny. Is anybody who really believes in New-Agey stuff — **Conversations with God**, for instance, seriously, or **The Celestine Prophecy**, or *any* of those dumb-shit books — are *any* of those people going to read this and go, *oh whoah, oh my God* — I doubt it. I don't think it's going to have any effect on what people think of this New Age stuff. I just hope people think it's funny. It was fun to

write. Whitehead was a funny character to get into. I wrote it a long time ago, and I was younger then, and I was probably funnier then. So it's probably funnier than what I can write now, to be honest. It's meant to be sort of a balancing thing; as you said, one side is kind of dark and a little bit somber — maybe even a little bit sad, because it is about the deterioration of a really super meaningful relationship — and so the other one is just kind of silly and playful and ridiculous.

*BB: Autobiographical elements pop-up throughout your father's body of work, going back as far as the opening to his first novel, **Someone is Bleeding**, which is modeled after how he first met your mother on the beach. Much of that is further solidified by the biographical information you provide in the book. As you were reading your father's work as you were growing up, were you aware of those autobiographical elements in his fiction (from using family members names for characters to more overt biographical information like in his novel **Generations**)?*

MATHESON: Well, the one where it really jumps out is **What Dreams May Come** — because *it's us*. It's *explicitly* us. I mean, there's *me*, and there's Ali, and there's Richard, and there's Tina. I mean, *there we are*. And there's Mom, and there's our dogs. That one — you couldn't *not* see it. Before that, I think I would have had an impressionistic sense, reading my Dad's stuff, of like, just a vague understanding of, *he's writing himself, here*. I mean, *this is Dad — I'm reading Dad*. I'm reading Dad's inner life, in ways that I really didn't understand exactly, but I was downloading him, in a way.

BB: You mention how your father told you near the end of his life how he felt that he was never close to anyone, and that he didn't understand other people. Do you think his writing was a means to attempt to address that?

MATHESON: I think it's a limitation in his writing that he doesn't write other people very well. I think he tends to write that guy at the center of the story pretty vividly

— pretty goddamn well. I mean like Neville (**I Am Legend**), and Scott Carey (**The Shrinking Man**), and Tom Wallace (**Stir of Echoes**) — Hackermeyer in **The Beardless Warriors** . . .

BB: Richard Collier . . .

MATHESOM: . . . Richard Collier (**Bid Time Return**), Chris Nielsen (**What Dreams May Come**), all of them. He writes those guys well, but I don't know if he wasn't interested in other people, or if he just didn't understand how to understand them. I don't think other people made a lot of sense to him, because what he said to me is, "I've never understood other people. I don't understand their inner lives. I never have." And I think that's true. I think that was basically him. And I think it bothered him. It bothered him — he wanted to talk about it. He didn't know what to do about it, and he was very old — he was 87 years-old. He didn't know what to do with it.

In terms of was his writing a way of reaching out, trying to make contact with other people, I mean it probably always is for every writer, in a way. I suppose you're trying to talk to other people; communicate with other people, so in a way, sure.

*BB: I think you nailed it when you pointed out that he was so talented at writing **the individual** — write what you know, right? You can literally step through each of the books, and find **him** in it.*

MATHESON: Yeah. And where is a character that is *not* him? Where does that exist? In his entire body of work. I would say the neighbor in **I Am Legend** . . .

BB: Ben Cortman.

MATHESON: Yeah. Cortman. Kind of, but not *really*. Not actually.

BB: Cortman, who reminds Neville of Oliver Hardy, which ties back in to his love of comedians . . .

MATHESON: Yeah, he has a weird death scene, where the new vampires are shooting him, and he's dying in slow-motion, and Neville feels sorry for him. But you know who cuts through? Who actually is alive, other than him? Dogs. Look at the dog in **I Am Legend**, and look at Katie in **What Dreams May Come**. And look at Ginger in **What Dreams May Come**. They're alive. And I would say my Mom kind of comes to life; that scene — that wild, weird scene at the end of **What Dreams May Come** — she's pretty specific; he gets kind of close to my Mom in that scene. Her strangeness, and her suspiciousness. It's not bad. That may be a high-watermark, I would say, for another human being, other than him. And maybe that's the only time he writes her with any real specificity. The wives in **The Shrinking Man** and **Stir of Echoes**, they're on the saintly side. They're sympathetic, as is the wife in **I Am Legend**. I'll tell you who's a fucking vivid character — an *amazing* character — but not in a very good way, I don't think, is 'Lover' in "Lover When You're Near Me." Oh shit, that's a hell of a character, but god damn it's *so* grotesquely misogynistic. It's like, "Oh Dad, oh my God, *Dad* — you can't write that! I know it's 1954, but whatever, you *can't* write that!"

*BB: There's a nice passage at the end of the memoir in which you mention that if your Dad was right, the two of you may end up arguing about the afterlife **in** the afterlife. That got me thinking about the postscript to your father's book **Bid Time Return**. Robert Collier, the brother of the main character Richard, refers to the manuscript describing how his brother traveled back in time to find the woman he loved. He goes on to say that he won't go looking for the proof that his brother did what is described, in the chance that it might not be there, leaving things with the hope that what his brother described truly happened. Having the luxury of being so far removed, I can look at your father's spiritual beliefs and say, even though I don't share them, if they provided him comfort about passing from this life, then that's not necessarily a bad thing. Do you take any solace from the fact that his beliefs may have helped him in the end?*

MATHESON: I don't, personally, not at all. Because I look at it a different way, which is those beliefs cut him off from what I would consider to be more real life. I don't know, did they comfort him? Who knows. Does anybody really truly in their heart of hearts believe that stuff when there's *absolutely* no evidence for it? And he'd say, *well there **is** evidence*. But it was always just bullshit. There's nothing real about it. That ridiculous bibliography at the end of **What Dreams May Come** is just a bunch of 'books by believers' essentially. There's no proof.

Do I think it helped him? No — I wish he hadn't. He was *cool*, man. He was a cool dude, my Dad. You know, he was funny, and he was talented. And he was this *big*, *strong, athletic* man who was *alive*, and he could *laugh,* and he could *play*. He was great. And this stuff just imprisoned him, in my book. I don't think it helped him. I don't personally think it helps anybody, myself. I think *live*, man. Live. We're *here.* Live, and don't wait for this imaginary reality you're going to go to, and think that that's better. *That's* the point. That somehow *this* isn't the point. We *definitely* had that conversation. I'm like, Dad, I think *this* is the point. What we're doing *right now. This* is the point — not that *other* thing. That other *made up* thing.

I don't know. Maybe I'm wrong. Do I think it made him feel better? Yeah, it probably comforted him. Because he was really scared of death. He was really, really, really, really scared of death. He was really scared of dying.

BB: *Has the experience of writing your memoir helped you, either in making sense of your relationship with your father, or at least allowing you to make peace with it? Has it done for you what you had hoped when you set out to write it?*

MATHESON: Yeah, I think so. It was great to spend time with my Dad again, you know? We had a strange journey. We were really, really, really close until I was like 25-26 years old. It's a long time. You know, like really close. We spent a *lot* of time together. A lot of beautiful moments.

And then — a pretty rapid deterioration, followed by maybe a three-year transition, I don't know, followed by twenty-five years that were *not* very good. They were contentious, and argumentative, and not very pleasant. And kind of chilly. I really loved the guy. I really do hope that comes through . . .

BB: *It does.*

MATHESON: I did. I loved him dearly. I didn't really have anyone else in my family. I don't think anybody else was happy I was there. I was the youngest one, and I don't think there were a lot of emotional resources to go around, to tell you the truth. I don't think they were happy with the arrival of the fourth kid — at all — but *he* was. *He* was happy that I was there, and man, I just adored him. But then we lost that. It sort of just frittered away. And so to go back, and feel like I was spending time with him — the nature of that kind of writing; that kind of dialogue is channeling him, obviously. And remembering some of the really beautiful things from my childhood and my teens; and re-playing what happened. Playing the whole thing out, I would say that on a personal level it was a very deep and moving experience, and I did get out of it what I was hoping to.

• • •

Readers interested in a deeper insight into the author of so many classic works across multiple mediums and genres will definitely want to pick up **Conversations with the Father**. *The more familiar you are with Matheson's works, the more you will appreciate the added insight into the man behind them that Chris' memoir provides.*

Conversations with the Father:
  A Memoir about Richard Matheson,
  My Dad and God
by Chris Matheson
Pitchstone Publishing
ISBN: 978-1634312325
Publication Date: July 19, 2022

Illustration by Carl Burgos (Justice, January 1956)

THE RETRIAL
Verdict Crime Detection Magazine 1956/57
by Richard Krauss

The 1953 four-issue run of *Verdict* was largely reprints, complementing *Manhunt*'s all-original-stories concept nicely. The idea must have continued to strike a chord with the publisher, because the idea carried forward in its 1956 reboot.

The second run, with the full title of *Verdict Crime Detection Magazine*, began in August 1956 with editorial director Walter R. Schmidt, managing editor William Manners, associate editor N.F. King, and art director Charles W. Adams, along with his assistant Gerald Adams.

Production values were sparse. All three covers repurposed the same Tom O'Sullivan art drawn as an interior illustration for *Manhunt* (Sept. 1955), with only the text and background color to differentiate one issue from the next. The reboot's paltry interior artwork was either thumbnail-sized sketches that appeared next to story titles or nothing at all. At least one is signed by Ray Houlihan, and judging by his style, he may well have drawn all of them.

Now let's dig into the individual issues themselves:

Verdict Crime Detection Magazine Vol. 1 No. 1
August 1956, 128 pages, 35¢

"Hanged Him in the Mornin'" by Craig Rice (7400 words)
Georgiana Ann Randolph Craig (1908–1957) wrote under the name Craig Rice, a combination of her parents' last name and the last name of Mr. and Mrs. Elton Rice, her paternal aunt and uncle who raised her and are credited with first stirring her interest in mysteries from readings of Edgar Allan Poe's stories and poems.

Craig's most famous character, John J. Malone, was introduced in a series of novels, beginning in 1939. The wise-cracking Chicago lawyer tackles his cases more like a sleuth than a solicitor, relying as much on serendipity as smarts when solving his improbable cases. ThrillingDetective.com labels his adventures screwball noir or hard-boiled farce. He drinks like Nick Charles, flirts with anything wearing a skirt, and practices law just short of shysterhood. "Not only had the jury been composed of hard-working, poverty-stricken men who liked nothing better than to convict a rich young wastrel of murder, but worse still, they'd all been too honest to be bribed."

Time magazine's January 28, 1946 cover story about Rice lists her at the top of her field. "The ceiling for detective stories is 20,000 copies (it

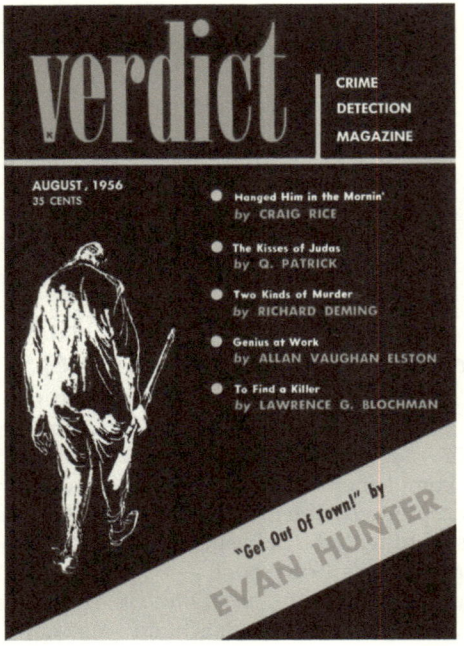

was somewhat lower before the war). Any author who sells in the 15,000 to 20,000 bracket [as Rice does,] is tops. In this bracket are writers like Erle Stanley Gardner, Raymond Chandler, Ellery Queen, Rex Stout, Mabel Seeley, Mignon Eberhart, [and] Craig Rice." Small wonder her stories frequently appeared in *Manhunt* and other top-selling digests.

John J. Malone made his debut in **Eight Faces at Three** (aka **Death at Three**) in 1939, the first of a dozen novels, and also starred in a slew of short stories. His first being "His Heart Could Break," a novelette first published in *Ellery Queen's Mystery Magazine* in March 1943. The story concerns Malone's client, a rich young wastrel who's just been granted a new trial, but is discovered hanging from a rope in his jail cell. After he's cut down, he's barely strong enough to whisper a single clue into Malone's ear before he passes. "It wouldn't break," he gasps.

Between glasses and bottles of rye, scotch, beer, and gin, Malone sweeps through his dead client's closest connections while an elusive melody haunts his inebriated brain. The lyrics waft through the narrative from page to page as if they hold the missing piece to

the puzzle. If only he could remember the words. Of course, at last he does and voilà, he's solved the murder. He rounds up the cast and conveniently delivers the verdict in the warden's office at the prison. It's a tightly plotted, tipsy romp that opens the return of *Verdict* under the title "Hanged Him in the Mornin'." The same story under its original title, "His Heart Could Break," also helped kick off the debut issue of *Verdict*'s first run in 1953! The story saw three additional reprints in *The Mysterious Traveler Magazine* (June 1942), *The Saint Mystery Magazine* (June 1959), and *Edgar Wallace Mystery Magazine* (March 1966), besides its foreign reprints.

"Get Out of Town!" by Evan Hunter (9450 words)

Salvatore Lombino (1926–2005) wrote under the names Evan Hunter, Ed McBain, Hunt Collins, Richard Marsten, and several others. He needed them because he wrote so much he often had more than one story in the same magazine and the editors didn't want to run the same name twice in an issue. In fact, this issue of *Verdict* provides just such an example. Directly following this story by Hunter is one by Collins.

A sailor and his best buddy get shore leave in Panama City. They cut loose at *The Paradise* bar where Frank disappears into one of the rooms upstairs with a "date." For Dave, an hour is too long for Frank to be gone; but then add on another 30 minutes, and Dave feels he must get to the bottom of things. Finding his way upstairs without a "date" and then locating Frank's shag suite is a short story in itself, but when Dave finally enters the room, he finds no trace of his pal or the young woman who led him astray. The hunt for Frank and wrapping up the damage Dave causes along the way makes a great story. Hunter provides plenty of Navy nuisance and Panama atmosphere to immerse readers in the time and place of the escapade.

"Where would Frank go? I knew the guy like a knew my own brother. We'd been through boots at Great Lakes together, we'd been to Radar School together out on Treasure Island, and we'd been assigned to the Hanfield together, having

to run away the hell up to Boston to pick up the ship. We'd been inseparable all through that, and I could tell when Frank was going to sneeze almost before he had the inclination himself."

"Eye-Witness" by Hunt Collins (1200 words)

Salvatore Lombino changed his legal name to Evan Hunter in 1952, around the same time he began working as an editor at the Scott Meredith Literary Agency. The job marked the beginning of his professional writing career. His breakout novel, **The Blackboard Jungle** in 1954, paved the way for a long, successful legacy.

His story, "Eye-Witness" was copyright 1952 by Picture Magazines, Inc. which suggests *Verdict*'s presentation was a reprint. It's a four-page setup built on a twist ending that unfortunately didn't come as a complete surprise. Its opening blurb explains: "He had witnessed a brutal murder, but to identify the killer would cause still another death!"

Despite its one-note premise, Collins/ Hunter's writing is engaging, and he imbues each character in his limited cast with their own quirks and slants.

"'I won't talk to anyone but the Chief,' he said. His eyes met mine for an instant, and then turned away. He was not being stubborn, I decided. I hadn't seen stubbornness in his eyes. I'd seen fear."

"To Find a Killer" by Lawrence G. Blochman (6500 words)

This reprint from the June 1, 1930 edition of *Adventure* was retitled from "Red Wine" for its appearance in *Verdict*. Lawrence Goldtree Blochman (1900–1975) leveraged his epicurean expertise and his knowledge of Asia, where he'd traveled extensively as a correspondent, for this story. His description of the setting on the isle of Tanjong Samar and the elaborate feast of the climax provide readers with an authentic taste of Indonesian culture and cuisine.

"They threaded their way among carved, high stemmed praus, drawn up on the beach, with red and blue demons grinning from their leaning masts. The two white men crawled

under the palm thatched canopy shading the middle of a long narrow sampan. Paddles dug into the brown water, churning the current. The craft swung upstream."

Private investigator Paul Vernier is tasked with uncovering a killer hiding among three Americans employed at the remote Kota Bharu rubber plantation. None of the three men match the description of Jerome Steeks, but Vernier is certain one of them is the murderer. He must use his wits to identify the killer and take him back to Batavia for trial.

Besides his career as a journalist, Blochman wrote some 30 mystery/ detective novels, often set in foreign lands like India, Japan, or Central America. Several were adapted for movies. He also wrote TV and radio scripts, hundreds of short stories, and translated French fiction—most notably **Three Beds in Manhattan** by Belgian George Simenon.

"Holdup!" by Don Stanford (1100 words)

Galactic Central lists only one other mystery story for Don Stanford, "One Little Thing You Forgot," for *Alfred Hitchcock's Mystery Magazine* (Aug. 1966). However, he sold plenty of work to upscale markets like *Redbook, Argosy, Cosmopolitan, Reader's Digest,* etc.

His *AHMM* story appears to be longer than this three-pager for *Verdict*, a short-short whose crux centers on an ex-cop's knowledge of law enforcement.

Donald Kent Stanford (1918–1992) was born in Chattanooga, Tennessee, and received his formal education at the Drexel Institute of Technology, Foreign Service Institute, and the University of Paris. Dick Knudson, of MossMotoring.com, describes Stanford as "a literary nomad who moved about on various continents supporting himself by writing novels, short stories, film and TV scripts."

Perhaps his most famous novel was **The Red Car,** which he wrote for Funk & Wagnall's over a summer in the early 1950s. It's a car-lover's dream about a Regency Red MG TC-series roadster aimed at the young adult market. Scholastic Books bought it, and brought it through several printings, culminating in estimated sales of over two million copies.

"Two Kinds of Murder" by Richard Deming (9300 words)

A reprint of "Two Tins of Murder" from *Bluebook* (Sept. 1952), this story concerns a drug smuggler whose front is an import business. His secretary first stumbles across his cache of cocaine-laden sardine cans and then stumbles across his corpse. And like every prime suspect in a 1960s *Perry Mason* episode on TV, she immediately picks up the murder weapon and is promptly spotted by an eye witness—in this case a policeman responding to a report of gunfire.

The patsy's fiancé enlists the aid of his childhood friend, Rock Swade. Swade, who denies he's a private investigator, is described by the local paper as a "fixer" with connections on both sides of the law. He works his contacts to gain an interview with the incarcerated secretary and plods on until he finally uncovers the real murderer amongst his gangland cronies, and saves the day.

I've read other Deming stories I liked better than this one. Too many pages are spent setting up events, and the exposition subjugates the action. The smattering of characterization is thin, yielding little concern for the accused and her boyfriend, the fixer, or even the gangsters vying for territory.

Richard Deming (1915–1983) wrote dozens of stories that were published in every crime digest you can think of. His series characters include vice cop Matt Rudd and P.I. Manny Moon. His pseudonyms include Max Franklin, Halsey Clark, Nick Morino, and Robert Hart Davis.

"Vengeance Is Mine" by Samuel Blas (2400 words)

This unforgettable, brutal crime story with a sickening twist shows what a brilliant writer can do in the space of just a few pages. The story originally saw print in *Collier's* January 11, 1947, as "Revenge" and the *Verdict* crew liked it so much they ran it in the July 1953 issue from the first run [see *bare•bones* No. 4, page 39],

changed the title, and ran it again here.

The story was adapted for TV for *Alfred Hitchcock Presents* (Oct. 2, 1955) and included in the anthology **Alfred Hitchcock Presents: A Baker's Dozen of Suspense Stories** (Dell, 1949).

"Kisses of Judas" by Q. Patrick (6800 words)

Another strong entry, "Judas" relates the story of two chums at boarding school. Our narrator, Pat, suffers only the usual childhood humilities, but his pal, Martin, gets his by the lorry load. His well-intentioned, but clueless father, who "suffered from a terrible disease of the throat which made every syllable he uttered a pathetic mockery of the English language," insists on lecturing his son and his schoolmates frequently and insufferably.

Over winter break, Martin invites Pat to stay at his home, where the latter witnesses firsthand the twisted lad's demeaning treatment by his oblivious pater. One slight leads to another and snowballs into tragedy—a real crime—for its victims may never move beyond its aftermath.

Engaging prose and character depth help camouflage the story's conveniently constructed elements to deliver a first-rate account of the perfect crime. The story first appeared in *Harper's Magazine* (April 1942) as "Portrait of a Murderer."

Q. Patrick was the pseudonym of the writing team of Richard Wilson Webb (1901–1970) and Hugh Callingham Wheeler (1912–1987). The pair's prolific output appeared frequently in *Detective Story Magazine* during the pulp era and in *Ellery Queen's Mystery Magazine* during the heyday of digests.

"Genius at Work" by Allan Vaughan Elston (1400 words)

A four-pager about a mystery writer who cranks out his potboilers on a typewriter in an office building he shares with realtors, insurance agents, accountants, and a dentist. Originally from *The American Magazine* (August 1949), titled "Do Not Disturb." Its payoff is well worth the build-up, but I won't spoil the fun by giving things away in this synopsis.

Allan Vaughan Elston (1887–1976) wrote western and detective fiction for pulps and digests from 1929 to 1951. He also sold scripts to anthology TV series like *Alfred Hitchcock Presents, Schlitz Playhouse, Robert Montgomery Presents,* etc. His work migrated from short stories to western novels, beginning with **Come Out and Fight** (Doubleday, 1941) and continued until his death in 1976.

"Ride for a Stranger" by David C. Cooke (1050 words)

Longstanding routines and the small town folk familiar with them help save the day in this three-page drama about a hitchhiker and a patsy. The author, David Coxe Cooke, wrote about a dozen crime stories for *The Saint Detective Magazine, Manhunt, Private Detective,* and a few others.

"The Deadly Sisters" by Samuel Elkin (4400 words)

On a visit to The Big Apple, spinster sisters, Eva and Dora, fall under the spell of grifter Paul Sheparton. He's well aware of their inherited fortune and plans to have it for himself. Too bad his phony lovemaking is documented by his own hand in his diary, recovered by the police after his murder. Who killed him? Was it Eva or Dora—or both?

This appears to be the first of only a few crime stories written by Elkin. It was reprinted as "Survival of the Fittest" in *Ellery Queen's Mystery Magazine* (Jan. 1960).

SUMMARY

Overall, a solid issue of *Verdict*'s return to the newsstand. However, it seems a bit odd the stories by Rice and Blas were included since they had already appeared in *Verdict*'s first unsuccessful run. In August 1956 *Verdict* shared the newsstand with *Accused* (July), *Crime and Justice* (Sept.), *Double-Action Detective, Ellery Queen, Guilty* (July), *Homicide* (Sept.), *Hunted, Jonathan Press Mystery, Manhunt, Mantrap* (July), *Mercury Mystery* (July), *Michael Shayne* (Sept.), *Murder!* (Sept.), *Pursuit* (July), *The Saint, Suspect,* and *Trapped.* Too much competition for most to survive.

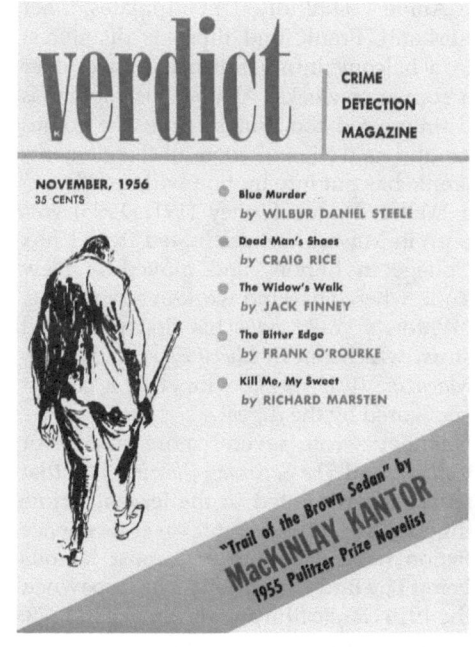

verdict CRIME DETECTION MAGAZINE

NOVEMBER, 1956
35 CENTS

Blue Murder
by WILBUR DANIEL STEELE

Dead Man's Shoes
by CRAIG RICE

The Widow's Walk
by JACK FINNEY

The Bitter Edge
by FRANK O'ROURKE

Kill Me, My Sweet
by RICHARD MARSTEN

"Trail of the Brown Sedan" by MacKINLAY KANTOR 1955 Pulitzer Prize Novelist

Like the other titles in St. John's line, the page fillers in *Verdict* were short true crime reports with titles like "Spooky Swag," "Spare and Rod," and "By Hook or Crook."

Verdict Crime Detection Magazine Vol. 1 No. 2 November 1956, 128 pages, 35¢

"The Widow's Walk" by Jack Finney (3100 words)

An elderly woman in poor health moves in with her son and his wife. The spouse, Annie, soon grows to despise her mother-in-law and plots her murder, suffocating the old woman with a pillow. She imagines the crime in great detail, but somehow her intended victim won't go easily.

"It's infuriating, though. So perfect, so simple—and I just can't do it." Annie abandons the idea until she thinks of something better. A simple push from a place high enough to ensure a fatal fall. But where? Their house offers no opportunities.

A magazine provides the answer: a widow's walk; named for the balconies where the wives of whalers perched to watch for the return of their husbands from the sea. The casualty rate of whalers was so high, the little porches were dubbed "widow walks."

Annie skillfully manipulates her husband, Frank, and flips his disinterest in a balcony into a finished project over a course of weeks. At first, his mother is disinterested too, but in time she comes around as well, and soon all the elements Annie has put into motion will tumble.

Walter Braden Finney (1911–1995) was born in Milwaukee, graduated from Knox College in Illinois, and moved to New York, where he found work in advertising. "Widow's Walk" was his first published story, which ran in *Ellery Queen's Mystery Magazine* (July 1947), winner of a contest sponsored by the digest.

Finney wrote several more stories for *Collier's* and *The Saturday Evening Post* that were later reprinted in the leading crime digests. He also wrote several science fiction novels, perhaps his most famous being **The Body Snatchers**, which spawned the 1956 classic film and its remake in 1978. He was awarded the World Fantasy Award for Life Achievement in 1987.

"The Bitter Edge" by Frank O'Rourke (3700 words)

This *Verdict* original traces the sorry paths of two underachievers as they collide in a desperate bid to find meaning in their lives. Charley Forbes is a two-time loser at love. When he turns to the bottle for solace, a painful ulcer forces sobriety against his bitter grudgement.

When the "Kentucky Kid" robs a bank and escapes to the wilderness, Charley is enlisted to assist in the manhunt. During the chase, Charley confronts his own demons.

Frank O'Rourke (1916–1989) wrote a handful of mystery stories, but is better known for his western fiction. Movies based on his novels include **The Bravados** (1958), **The Professionals** (1966) based on **A Mule for the Merquesa**, and **The Great Bank Robbery** (1969). Later in life, he wrote children's literature. His wife was painter Edith Carlson O'Rourke (1923–2007).

"Blue Murder" by Wilbur Daniel Steele (7200 words)

The end reveal was the best thing about this story. A detail that fleshed out suspicions formed early in its pages. It's a reprint from *Harper's Magazine* (October 1925). Three brothers, who once fancied the same pretty girl, have settled into their roles as farmer, shopkeeper, and blacksmith. The farmer got the girl and returns home with a wild horse, a steed named Blue Murder that once killed a man.

You don't have to like characters to like reading about them. Too bad, this lot is painted in broad strokes, neither engaging nor intriguing. In today's parlance, this would be rural noir I suppose, but more disappointingly a boring 18 pages. Still, the story saw print again and again in *EQMM*, *Verdict*, *Manhunt*, and *The Saint*. Go figure.

Wilbur Daniel Steele (1886–1970) was an author and playwright. In **20th Century American Literature**, Martin Bucco called him "America's recognized master of the popular short story."

"Priest Hole" by Clayre & Michel Lipman (4600 words)

There are only five stories listed at Galactic Central for this writing pair, but if they're as good as this *Verdict* original, they're worth seeking out.

A smooth-talking shyster worms his way into a partnership with an old-school lawyer whose attention has drifted away from casework to research and monographs. While the old man writes histories, his younger partner builds the firm into big money. The captivating story of these two opposites pulls readers along until the older partner, now in failing health, uncovers the younger's nefarious deeds and plots a last bid for justice.

Clayre Lipman (1913–1978) and her husband Michel (Martin) Lipman (1913–2010) wrote one novel together, **House of Evil** (1954) that was reprinted in **A Trio of Lions** by Stark House Press (2016). They also wrote a three-act play, *The Night We Ate Aunt Minnie*, in 1943. After Clayre's death in 1978, Michel turned to writing books for children and young adults. His works include **You Are the Mayor, You Are the Judge, You Are the Justice, How to Write Clearly**, and several others.

"Kill Me, My Sweet" by Richard Marsten (3900 words)

A blatantly adulterous wife plots the murder of her wealthy husband in this character study of measured tension and repulsion. It originally ran in the men's magazine *Real* (Nov. 1954) and makes a perfect *Verdict* reprint. Marsten includes two nice twists, the first unexpected, the second less so.

Richard Marsten was another pseudonym of Evan Hunter (1926–2005). Under it, he sold stories to all the best hardboiled crime digests like *Manhunt*, *Accused*, *Pursuit*, and suspense-champion *Hitchcock*.

"The Trail of the Brown Sedan" by MacKinlay Kantor (5750 words)

Shortly after the coppers successfully extradite murderer Rainy Moper, a brown sedan intercepts his transport to justice and opens fire. But rescue is not in the cards. The thugs mow down Moper along with three lawmen in a hail of machine gun fire.

After the setup, patrolman Nick Glennan, who is eventually joined by his brother Dave, tracks the crooks and their vehicle over a ten-page car chase with a few pit stops to interview witnesses and gather clues.

The Glennan brothers appeared in two other stories for *Detective Fiction Weekly* in the early 1930s. This story is from the January 6, 1934 issue. It may have still offered an exciting read in *Verdict*'s day, but as the story approaches its centennial, it's decided dated.

Benjamin MacKinlay Kantor (1904–1977) wrote dozens of crime stories for detective pulps from 1928 through 1936. He also found success in the "slicks" with sales to *Collier's*. His "Rogue's Gallery" for them is his most reprinted story. His pulp stories were not generally among his fond memories, but he once wrote that "Brown Sedan" "has a kind of sharpness and pungency not always found in pulp magazine material."

Kantor went on to write some fifty books of fiction and nonfiction in addition to his short fiction and magazine articles. His Civil War novel about an infamous Confederate prison camp, **Andersonville** (1955), was awarded the Pulitzer Prize for Fiction in 1956. In 1960, *Look* magazine published his short alternate history novel **If the South Had Won the Civil War**. It generated so much interest it was reprinted in paperback by Bantam the following year.

"Hangman's Witness" by Wade H. Mosby (3700)

This *Verdict* original may be its author's first published crime story.

"We all feel a passing pity for this sort of derelict [a person no one has ever loved], and the more sensitive of us experience a guilty twinge. Because we killed this man, not the executioner. Each of us, in some way, by doing or not doing, excluded this man from human warmth, as surely as if he were pounding at that door right now and none of us was willing to forego a moment of comfort to let him in."

Our narrator, Joe Morely, spins an engaging tale of love won and lost. The impervious strength that forges the bonds of friendship is so strong it binds two men together even when one betrays the other.

Mosby weaves a compelling character study of two men's lives. At first inseparable, but in time growing distant; yet through it all they remain in each other's grip. Morely's audience consists of three men engaged for a dinner party in the dead of winter at his home. As Morely lays bare his secrets, readers at last learn the reason for his mysterious invitation.

Wade H. Mosby (1917–2005) served in the United States Army during WWII. During his over 30 years of employment at the *Milwaukee Journal*, he served as editor of the paper's Green Sheet section. The four-page daily section, printed on green paper, carried the paper's entertainment features, including its comics. Mosby interviewed Al Vermeer about his popular comic strip *Priscilla's Pop* for the Green Sheet in 1970. Mosby wrote short stories from time to time, from 1956 through the 1980s for *EQMM*, *AHMM*, and *Mike Shayne*. He also sold at least one to *Boy's Life*, "Dark, Dank, and Dismal" (Oct. 1961).

"Dead Men's Shoes" by Craig Rice (6700 words)

Investigative lawyer John J. Malone makes his second and final appearance in *Verdict*'s second run. It first saw print in *Baffling Detective Mysteries* (July 1943) and *EQMM* (March 1948) before inclusion here.

From his barstool, Malone hears tell of an inauspicious fellow named B.L. (Bad Luck) Bradley whose reputation surpasses his circle of actual acquaintances. The little lawyer soon learns nobody wants help from Bradley; for, once bestowed, the recipient disappears off the face of the Earth.

Malone's casual interest in Bradley is interrupted when a beautiful young woman sits down at the bar next to him. When she calls the bartender over and asks, "Who's Bad Luck Bradley?" the mystery deepens. It's all a tangled, amusing mix of fakers and gossamer threads, with only Malone savvy enough to unravel the mystery's underlying scam.

During his dubious exploration of what's what, Malone cajoles his pal, Homicide Captain Daniel von Flanagan, into the muddle; much to the detective's regret. But all is forgiven when the little lawyer finally produces a bona fide crime and its perp.

As noted earlier, Craig Rice was among the elite mystery writers of her day. She even edited her own magazine, *The Craig Rice Mystery Digest*, a one-shot published by Bond-Charteris in 1945. The volume doubled as No. 12 of the Bonded series that includes several *The Saint's Choice* volumes. It features four abridged reprints.

When Anson Bond sold his partnership with Leslie Charteris to Rudy Vallee for $100,000, he went on to form Anson Bond Publications. Continuing with a minor name change, the *Craig Rice Crime Digest* went for two additional issues during the second half of 1946. Each issue included mystery novels condensed to just 18,000 words by famous authors such as Carter Dickson, Richard Powell, and Lawrence Treat.

Rice served as a ghostwriter for actor George Sanders, whom she met while working on screenplays for two of The Falcon movies. Rice also did the early work on the screenplay for *Lady of Burlesque*, the Barbara Stanwyck movie based on **The G String Murders**, written as a novel by Gypsy Rose Lee.

"The Shadow on the Hill" by David C. Cooke (6050 words)

Chasing cheating spouses may pay the bills, but when the promise of a case a little more interesting walks into PI Greg Chambers' office, he ignores his better judgement and takes the case. His new client's abrupt manner was the first red flag. But the offer of a thousand-dollar retainer, along with full disclosure after accepting the stranger's invitation to move into his home for protection, is too much for Chambers to resist.

The client, copper tycoon Harry Bradford, has received an anonymous death threat and needs Chambers to find out who sent it and stop them. Chambers gets busy the moment he arrives at Bradford's mansion and soon weeds out the top suspects from among the support staff. But earning his fee won't be easy or straightforward.

"Shadow" first appeared in the pulp *Private Detective* (May 1950). David Coxe Cooke (1917–2000) wrote about a dozen stories for pulps and digests throughout the 1950s. He often served as editor for the annual **Best Detective Stories of the Year** from 1947 through 1957. His non-fiction books covered topics like aeronautics, Asia, fitness, and sports.

"Bridge Game" by Bryce Walton (5000 words)

For such a prodigious author, I was surprised at how little I could find out about Bryce Walton (1918–1988), who wrote a great deal of crime and science fiction shorts and novels. He wrote scripts for the *Captain Video and His Video Rangers* television series and for six episodes of *Alfred Hitchcock Presents*; some based on his fiction. During WWII, he served as a Navy correspondent and attended California State College beginning in 1946. I thought he may have studied psychiatry there as it figures largely in this story, but I found no evidence of his major.

He wrote about the topic convincingly

in this *Verdict* original. In therapy, Dr. Bernstein helps Laurene Leland figure out what's wrong with her marriage. She wed a father figure rather than a lover. Now she's stuck with "a detached scientists type, a bore and a cold fish if ever there was one."

Her true love, a lawyer named Hal, swears he can get anyone off, and proves it when Laurene shoots her husband at a party in plain sight of several witnesses—Hal included! The conniving lawyer plunks his magic twanger, the case is dismissed, and Laurene is institutionalized. And that's as far as so good goes. The rest is decidedly more just and less lenient.

SUMMARY

Another solid, enjoyable issue. The *Verdict* originals were all consistently strong, while the quality of the reprints spanned a wider range. That said, there's enough excellence here to make this issue a worthy addition to any crime fiction collector's library.

Verdict Crime Detection Magazine Vol. 2 No. 1 January 1957, 128 pages, 35¢

"Foot of the Cliff" by Frank O'Rourke (5100 words)
A vacation in Acapulco does nothing to reverse the trajectory of the marriage of Shane and Marion on its long spiral to Hell. She's a shameless cheat, and he's a drunkard. So far, their marriage still hangs by a thread. But when Marion chances across service man Charley, on his first big leave from duty, things are about to break.

First published in the pages of *Esquire* (Nov. 1947), "Cliff" is a character study of defeatism and cynical thinking. Frank O'Rourke (1916–1989) wrote over 100 stories. This crime story is a rare break from his usual western yarns. He wrote one novel, **Instant Gold** (1964) as Frank O'Malley.

"Tiger in the Kitchen" by James M. Cain (6800)
"Things first began to go sour between Duke and Lura when they put in the cats. They didn't need no cats. They had a combination auto-camp, filling-station,

and lunchroom out in the country a ways, and they got along all right." In the vernacular of our narrator, the hired man tells his tale of salacious dysfunction through a countrified inflection native to somewheres rural in the Golden State.

The felines began as mere wildcats but soon Duke brung in a mountain lion and before he was done had hisself a real live tiger name of Rajah. He claimed he wasn't afraid of them cats, but he would'a been crazy not to be. Unlike Lura, who had a natural affinity with them. It's true, Wild Bill Smith, a traveling snake oil salesman, had read it in the palm of Lura's hand.

When Duke took off on another one of his trips carrying on and whatnot, 'ol Bill and Lura had more time to get better acquainted. Before you knowed it, Lura's expectin' and then deliverin' and by the time Duke figures out the baby ain't his, well, let's just say the only tiger in the kitchen weren't Lura.

"Tiger" was first published in *The American Mercury* (Jan. 1933) as "The Baby in the Icebox."

James M. Cain (1892–1977) left a lucrative career as a journalist behind and moved to Hollywood to write fiction. An agent helped him land a job with Paramount as a screenwriter in 1931. His first novel,

The Postman Always Rings Twice, was a groundbreaking success. It was followed by **Double Indemnity** (1936), **Serenade** (1937), **Mildred Pierce** (1941), and a dozen more in the decades to come. An anthology, **The Baby in the Icebox and Other Short Stories** appeared posthumously in 1981.

"Smee" by Ex-Private X (4750 words)

Alfred McLelland Burrage (1889–1956) wrote primarily children's stories for British magazines such as *Chums*, *Boys' Friend Weekly*, *Boys Herald*, and *Comic Life*. Under the name Frank Lelland he wrote numerous stories in the "Tufty" series. Tufty Fluffytail was a red squirrel character created in 1953 by Elsie Mills to promote road safety among children.

As Ex-Private X, the author wrote **War is War** (1930) a bitter war memoir. A.M. Burrage is perhaps best remembered for his ghost stories. Among his most famous are "The Green Scarf" (1927), "Between the Minute and the Hour" (1927), and "The Waxworks" (1931), which was adapted for episodes of *Lights Out* (1950) and *Alfred Hitchcock Presents* (1959).

"Smee" is also a ghost story and originally published in *Nash's — Pall Mall Magazine* (Dec. 1929). On Christmas Eve, a party of fourteen gathered "with just the proper leavening of youth." After dinner, a suggestion to engage in a nostalgic game of hide-and-seek was enthusiastically embraced by all save a young man named Jackson. He outright refused to play. When pressed, he explained he had visited a house where a girl had died while playing the game. A door that seemed the entrance to a bedroom led in fact to a back stairway. The girl plunged inside and fell, breaking her neck as she plummeted to the bottom.

For some reason, Jackson suggested a derivative game called Smee. (A conjunction of the phrase "It's me.") "Every player is presented with a sheet of paper. All the sheets are blank except one, on which is written 'Smee.' Nobody knows who is 'Smee' except 'Smee' himself—or herself, as the case may be. The lights are then turned out and 'Smee' slips from the room and goes off to hide, and after an interval the other players go off in search,

without knowing whom they are actually in search of. One player meeting another challenges with the word 'Smee' and the other player, if not the one concerned, answers 'Smee.'

"The real 'Smee' makes no answer when challenged, and the second player remains quietly by him. Presently they will be discovered by a third player who, having challenged and received no answer, will link up with the first two. This goes on until all the players have formed a chain, and the last to join is marked down a forfeit."

The group is game for a session, but again Jackson declines to join them. When pressed further to explain, he then recounts a round of Smee he once played in the same house where the girl had died while playing hide-and-seek. He was one of a group of a dozen players in that game of Smee, who spread out throughout the storied home, and as the participants linked up, the headcount grew inexplicably to thirteen!

A well-told ghost story, but quite predictable. How it fits into a crime detection magazine is the extent of its mystery.

"Death of a Lawman" by Borden Deal (3700 words)

One Sunday afternoon, a junior reporter is told to write a story about a local lawman named Kirby Rountree.

"'I started when I was twenty-five years old,' he [Rountree] said. 'I was a deputy sheriff right here in this office. I'll be seventy-five come October so that makes it right at fifty years.' He looked around the room. 'And now I'm deputy sheriff here again. I been sheriff twice, city marshal, was a state revenue man at one time. But one way and another I've spent my life at law-enforcement work.'"

The story evokes the rural south, where author Borden Deal spent much of his life. The veteran lawman gets a call to head out to Old Man Moats's place before he's able to parse out enough for a feature story, so the reporter goes with him—to talk further during the drive.

By the time they arrive at Moats' house, Rountree's provided enough background for a good character piece. This isn't the deputy's first visit to Moats' place. The man gets nasty when he's drunk. This time he's threatened to shoot his wife and son.

The story title of this *Verdict* original gives you the gist of where things are headed, but Deal tells the tale at a slow burn, and keeps you reading to catch the details.

Borden Deal (1922–1985) grew up poor during the Depression and his early years struggling in the Deep South are reflected in his work. In 1946, he attended the University of Alabama and published his first story, "Exodus." His professor of creative writing was the renowned Hudson Strode. Upon graduation, Deal moved on to Mexico City College for graduate study. By 1956, he decided to pursue a career as a full-time writer. His given name was Loysé Youth Deal, but he wrote as Alvin Winston, Loyse Deal, Lee Borden, Leigh Borden, and Michael Sunga. As Borden Deal, many of his short crime stories appeared in *Alfred Hitchcock's Mystery Magazine*, but he also sold a few to *Mercury Mystery*, *Mike Shayne*, *Ellery Queen*, and *The Saint*.

A prolific writer, Deal also sold to *McCall's*, *Collier's*, *Saturday Review*, and *Good Housekeeping*. He wrote twenty-one novels, including **The Insolent Breed**, **Dunbar's Cove**, and **The Tobacco Men**. He won the Guggenheim Fellowship (1957), an American Library Association Liberty and Justice award (1956), and an American Library Association Literary award (1963). Deal's second wife was author Babs Hodges.

"The Restless Corpse" by Norman Matson (8300 words)

The Harold Matson Company literary agency represented such heavyweights as Evelyn Waugh, C.S. Forester, and Flannery O'Connor. They held the copyright for this story, then called "Remains to Be Found," circa 1935. It's not clear whether its appearance in *Verdict* was a reprint or its first printing.

A newspaper reporter collaborates with Captain Horace Williams of the 13th Street police station to solve the mystery of a missing corpse, untangling a myriad of closely associated relationships of "persons of interest." It's a plum.

Norman (Haghejm) Matson (1893–1965) wrote nearly three dozen stories for top-paying markets like *Esquire*, *The Saturday Evening Post*, *The New Yorker*, *Mystery*, and several others. He was best known for completing the novel **The Passionate Witch** (1941) begun by Thorne Smith, who died before it was finished. Matson also wrote a sequel, **Bats in the Belfry** (1943). The film, *I Married a Witch* and the television series *Bewitched* were both loosely based on the books. Matson also wrote **Flecker's Magic** (1926) and **Doctor Fogg** (1929).

"Killer's Keeper" by David X. Manners (2800 words)

Verdict's introductory blurb incorrectly states: "This one became the Warner Brothers smash hit, **Conflict**, starring Humphrey Bogart." While often repeated online, it turns out that's not true. "Killer's Keeper" originally appeared in *Detective Fiction Weekly* April 27, 1940.

Two brothers compete for dominance. At least that's the way the one who always comes in second fiddle sees it. Fed up after losing the affections of Dolores, Jes figures if he can't beat brother Ken, maybe he should eliminate him. A commonplace setup is elevated nicely through satisfying prose and a couple of well-delivered twists.

David X. Manners (1912–2007) was a prolific author and editor. He wrote hundreds of short stories and dozens of books. During his career he served as an editor for *Popular Science* and *House Beautiful,* and was founder of a public relations agency doing business as David X. Manners Company.

"Recipe for Murder" by C. P. Donnel, Jr. (1650 words)

Inspector Miron interviews Madame Chalon, suspected of poisoning her first and second husbands. The widow freely admits her guilt, but the specifics of her method and the good Inspector's interest in it are quite unexpected. The story first appeared in *The American Legion Magazine* (Jan. 1947).

Cornelius Peter Donnel, Jr. (1906–1977) began his career as a police reporter and sold crime fiction to a variety of pulps and magazines, including *The Saturday Evening Post* and *Esquire*. His series characters, Walter "Doc" Rennie appeared in sixteen adventures for *Black Mask*, and Colonel Stephen Kaspir in fifteen for *Dime Detective Magazine*. His only novel, **Murder-Go-Round**, was published in 1945.

"Two Minutes" by William H. McMasters (3800 words)

What appears to be an iron-clad murder case against his client is shattered by an attorney through his careful cross-examination of the star witness for the prosecution. A well written *Verdict* original that hinges on a stilted bit of trickery orchestrated by the defense.

A rare short story by William H. McMasters (1877–1968) who served as Governor of South Dakota from 1921 to 1925. A publicist, playwright, and author who penned **Revolt: An American Novel** (1919). His most infamous client as a publicist was Charles Ponzi. When McMasters realized Ponzi was a conman, he exposed him in *The Boston Post*, winning the paper a Pulitzer Prize for the coverage in 1921. McMasters was never formally recognized for his role until he was awarded the Cliff Robertson Sentinel Award in 2011, posthumously, at the 22nd Annual Fraud Conference and Exhibition.

"Instrument of Torture" by Henry Slesar (4800 words)

Back in the days of land-lines, well before caller ID, a phone number could be an open channel to anonymous harassment. There wasn't much you could do other than change your number. And that's exactly what Maggi Landis does in this *Verdict* original. At first it did the trick, but as the story opens, Maggi's "friend" is back in full creep mode.

Maggi's boyfriend Larry talks things out with her, compiling a list of every suspect who knows her and could learn of her new number. The prime suspect is the middle-aged supervisor of the sales department where Maggi works.

"They say he makes passes at all the girls. The young girls. Everybody has some kind of story about him."

Larry decides to give the suspected phone stalker a taste of his own medicine and provides a case study in why it's not a good idea to take the law into your own hands.

Henry Slesar (1927–2002) wrote hundreds of stories for mystery and science fiction digests and scripts for radio and television. This telephone tale of terror calls up the spirit of the play (1952) and movie (1954) *Dial M for Murder*, written by Frederick Knott.

"Between Eight and Eight" by C.S. Forester (5550 words)

We all know we're going to die someday, but we try not to dwell on it. But what if you knew the exact time and place of your inevitable doom? That's what inmate Manners faces in his final twelve hours on death row. Forester delivers a brutal, realistic depiction of the agony of knowing, followed by a miraculous—yet believable—escape from prison and the manhunt that ensues. Manners eludes every obstacle in his path, save one.

A terrific story that first appeared in the Australian *Short Story Magazine* No. 32 (1947). A rare story to appear outside the usual haunts of *Ellery Queen* and *The Saint* for Cecil Lewis Troughton Smith (1899–1966), who wrote as C.S. Forester. In fact, it had also been reprinted earlier in *EQMM* (June 1950) and subsequently in *Ellery Queen's Anthology* No. 10 (1966).

Forester wrote plenty of short fiction and novels over his prolific career, including a twelve-book series about Horatio Hornblower (1950–1964). **The African Queen** (1935) was adapted into the classic film in 1951 under the direction of John Huston, and Forester's **The Good Shepherd** (1955) was adapted by and starred Tom Hanks as *Greyhound* (2020).

"You Can't Beat Routine" by J. W. Aaron (3550 words)

The issue's final story is a *Verdict* original with a satisfying finish. A crooked jeweler is confronted by a much different crime involving his wife.

"They found her car Friday afternoon, seven miles north of town, near a deserted farmhouse on a little-used gravel road. The interior of her distinctive little hardtop was blood-smeared. They found her clothes, ripped and torn and bloody, in the trunk. There was no sign of Grace."

Shock and horror transform into injury and anger when the jeweler discovers Grace has cleaned out their illicit stash and skipped town. So begins a methodical pursuit that eventually ends worse than it began.

John D. Bjorkman (1924–2004) wrote as J.W. Aaron for several of the best crime digests of the era, including *Trapped, Hitchcock, Manhunt,* and *Guilty.*

SUMMARY

During the final half of 1956, *Manhunt* publisher Michael St. John and general manager Richard E. Decker launched three new crime fiction digests to build on the success of their bestselling *Manhunt.* Unfortunately, none of the new titles lasted more than a few issues.

First up was *Mantrap,* in July 1956. Both of its covers featured photography rather than the traditional approach of paintings. The July issue displayed a "Body in Blue Jeans," and the final issue, in October, a woman screaming about something terrifying off-page.

In terms of longevity, *Murder!* was the most successful of three titles. It debuted in September 1956 and ended a year later, after five issues.

The final magazine was *Verdict,* a digest of an earlier life in 1953 [See Digging into Crime Digests in *bare•bones* No. 4.] Unlike the others, *Verdict* utilized reprints of classic crime stories. *Mantrap* and *Murder!,* like *Manhunt,* were published by Flying Eagle Publications. Although, by its third issue (March 1957), the indicia for *Murder!* switched to Fine Art Publications. The first two issues of *Verdict*'s second run were brought to newsstands through Secret Life Publications, but the final issue switched to Flying Eagle Publications.

Cross promotion ramped up slowly. I found no editorial announcements building excitement or awareness for any of the new titles prior to their launch. *Mantrap* was first mentioned in a postscript response to a letter of comment on the last page of *Manhunt,* Sept. 1956. That same month, an all-text ad appeared in the debut issue of *Murder!,* promoting the "big four" (*Manhunt, Verdict, Murder!,* and *Mantrap*). By October, the same ad began running in *Manhunt.*

Between *Verdict*'s two iterations, I'd give the earlier 1953 run the edge. Most obviously, for its superior cover art, but also its serialization of a novel—of which, Rex Stout's **Fer-de-Lance** was an excellent choice. The mix of top-notch reprints alongside a few originals seems a worthy formula and worked effectively in both series. Like the first outing, *Verdict*'s second run was a promising effort and unfortunately a likely casualty of too much competition. The second run of *Verdict* ends with a bang, its final issue surely a contender for the best of its last run.

•••

References

The Armchair Detective, Vol. 12 No. 4 Fall 1979, letter from Michael Masliah.

The Armchair Detective, Vol. 13 No. 3 Summer 1980, "Craig Rice: Merry Mistress of Mystery and Mayhem" by Mark Ann Grochowski.

A Trio of Lions page 303 Stark House Press 2016.

The Big Book of Espionage, edited by Otto Penzler, Vintage Crime, 2020.

The Big Book of Ghost Stories, edited by Otto Penzler, Vintage Books, 2012.

FantasticFiction.com

FindAGrave.com

Fraud-Magazine.com

Galactic Central website

GoodReads.com

ILovetheUpperWestSide.com

IMDb.com

LibraryThing.com

MossMotoring.com

MysteryFile.com

New York Times. January 23, 1975, page 36.

NostalgiaCentral.com

Paperback Confidential by Brian Ritt, Stark House Press, 2013.

SF-Encyclopedia.com

The [Stamford] *Advocate,* Jan. 30, 2007.

Time magazine, January 28, 1946 "Books: Mulled Murder, with Spice" cover story.

Wikipedia.com

MONSTERS UNLEASHED (AGAIN)!
The Marvel Horror Magazines, Part 2
by Peter Enfantino
with Gilbert Colon and Matthew R. Bradley

After *Dracula Lives* made a sizable ripple in the monster magazine newsstand of 1973, it was only natural that Marvel would further mine their stable of creatures for a second foray into the new territory. The first issue had no hint of that upcoming move, instead opting for adaptations, reprints, and a few originals. It was with the second issue that *Monsters Unleashed* perfected its personality.

Monsters Unleashed #1 (June 1973)
Cover by Gray Morrow

"The Man Who Cried Werewolf"
Story by Robert Bloch
Adaptation by Gerry Conway
Art by Pablo Marcos

"The Thing in the Freezer"
Story by Marv Wolfman
Art by Syd Shores

"Vampire Tale"
Story Uncredited
Art by Doug Wildey
(reprinted from *Journey Into Mystery* #16, June 1954)

"Skulls in the Stars"
Story by Robert E. Howard
Adaptation by Roy Thomas
Art by Ralph Reese

"One Foot in the Grave"
Story Uncredited
Art by Tony DiPreta
(reprinted from *Journey Into Mystery* #1, June 1952)

"The Fake"
Story Uncredited
Art by Al Eadah
(reprinted from *Menace* #10, March 1954)

"World Warlocks"
Story by Gardner Fox and Roy Thomas
Art by Gene Colan

Unlike *Dracula Lives!* and (the forthcoming) *Tales of the Zombie, Monsters Unleashed* begins life as an anthology book rather than a showcase for continuing characters. The overall sense here is one of bad management. I'm not sure enough time was spent on a game plan for the black and white line. *Monsters Unleashed,* for instance, is a hodgepodge of *Famous Monsters of Filmland* and *Creepy.* Bad puns and decently drawn half-nekkid women (but not enough edge to get them fully nekkid a la Warren) do not a successful venture make. The difference between Marvel and Warren in 1973 is that Warren's black and white comic magazines (*Creepy, Eerie* and *Vampirella*) had a pretty high quality writing percentage (particularly *Creepy*). Not so here.

I love Robert Bloch's short stories but "The Man Who Cried Wolf" is not one of his better works and that carries right over to the adaptation. It's a wholly predictable story of infidelity and female werewolves with passable PG-13 art by Pablo Marcos (in these B&Ws, all women have really big breasts and they're always busting those buttons) and not nearly as good as the Bloch adaptations to be found in the second iteration of *Journey Into Mystery*. "Thing"'s go from bad to the worst in Marv Wolfman's "Thing in the Freezer," an abominable bit of tripe about a zombie infestation on a cruise liner. Wolfman got his start selling crap like this at DC and, when he jumped ship, he brought his bag of cliches with him. Thankfully he'll show just how good he could be later on when his run on *Tomb of Dracula* really started cooking but, in the first issue of *MU*, he's still looking for his voice.

"Skulls in the Stars," Roy Thomas's adaptation of a Robert E. Howard Solomon Kane story reads more like one of Howard's fragments but it's graced with splendid Ralph Reese art. Can "World of Warlocks" save an otherwise unremarkable premiere issue? 'Fraid not. It's a John Carter, Warlord of Mars homage snoozefest that should probably have been scheduled for *Savage Tales*. Though its clear from the climax that PFC Brian Morgan, Warlord of Warlocks was being set up for a continuing

series, mercifully a second chapter was not forthcoming. The three reprints this issue are just as forgettable, but one is mildly amusing: "Vampire Tale" (which originally appeared in the pre-code *Journey Into Mystery* #16 in June 1954) concerns a very bandaged man who's put on trial for murdering a man he claims was a vampire. After he's found guilty and sentenced to death, he doffs bandages to reveal he's a rotting corpse, a victim of the vampire!

Tony Isabella provides a "jocular" run-down of the four Universal horror features starring Larry Talbot, The Wolfman. The adjective is in quotes because, aside from Isabella himself, I can think of no one who would find these jokes funny ("Ma and Pa Kettle Meet the Lycanthrope" anyone?). As for the piece itself, we get nothing more than a Forry Ackerman-style synopsis of the films. It's as if Isabella has no opinion on these films other than a one-liner or two.

Monsters Unleashed #2 (September 1973)
Cover by Boris Vallejo

"Frankenstein 1973"
Story by Gary Friedrich
Art by John Buscema and Syd Shores

"Karloff: The Man, The Monster, The Movies"
Book review by Tony Isabella

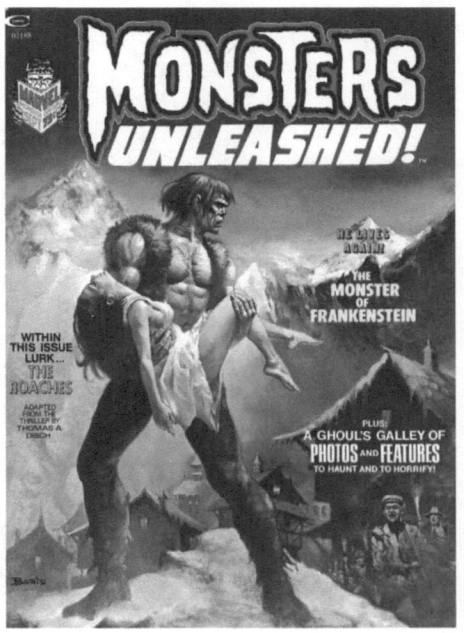

"Lifeboat"
Story by Gerry Conway
Art by Jesus Blasco

"The Madman"
Story by Stan Lee
Art by Bill Everett
(reprinted from *Menace* #4, June 1953)

"The World's Most Wanted Monster"
Text by Martin Pasko

"Sword of Dragonus"
Story by Frank Brunner and Chuck Robinson
Art by Frank Brunner
(reprinted from *Phase* #1, 1971)

"The Roaches"
Story by Gerry Conway
Adapted from the story by Thomas M. Disch
Art by Ralph Reese

Effective this issue, *Monsters Unleashed* becomes a Marvel Monster Vehicle, spotlighting a different MM each issue. This time out we get the Frankenstein Monster, magically transported to 1973. Boy wonder neuro-surgeon Derek McDowell has discovered that the sideshow freak floating in a tank of water is none other than the genuine Frankenstein's Monster. Derek decides he really must have the monster to experiment on but his gorgeous fiancé has other ideas. Believing the creature to be a rubber fake and not wanting it to come between her and her beau, she sets fire to the tent holding the monster's tank. Her plan goes awry when she, herself, is set ablaze and the monster is unleashed on the carnival grounds, killing scores until an army bazooka puts things right. Those, like me, who've been spoiled by the A+ job Gary Friedrich and Mike Ploog had been doing with the four-color *The Monster of Frankenstein* may find this contemporary version a bit jarring. John Buscema's one of Marvel's top artists but I'm not sure he belongs on this strip. There's a blandness to most of John's pencils here that you won't find on Buscema's run on *Conan the Barbarian* or *Fantastic Four*.

The story, nothing more than an incident, goes nowhere. McDowell's hippie slang feels forced and there's a not so subtle hint of misogyny (Derek backhands his fiancé and constantly berates her) that feels like it might be there just to take advantage of the "PG-13 rating" afforded the B&Ws. The flashback of the monster's history covers only the first four issues so it's up in the

air as to whether events that happen post-*Monster of Frankenstein* #4 will jibe with what's going on here or whether we'll ever get an explanation as to how the monster ended up in the carnival in the first place. Another Ajax bomb to throw into the discussion is the fact that, eventually, events in the four-color title will take place in our present as well. Alternate Frankenstein Monster Universes? We'll see.

"Lifeboat" is nothing in the way of original, patched together from all sorts of horror stories, but it's the most obvious example yet of where Marvel wanted to steer their new line of B&Ws. The company must have believed that, with the addition of European artists such as Esteban Maroto, Pablo Marcos, Alfredo Alcala, and Jesus Blasco (whose "Lifeboat" would be his only Marvel work) and the easing of restrictions the new CCA-less magazine line brought, a plundering of Warren's market share was on the horizon. Indeed, Blasco's fine pencil work (which reminded me of Warren mainstay Jose Bea) would have fit in rather well with Uncle Creepy and Cousin Eerie and the artist later found work at the competitor.

"The Madman" is a fun, if predictable, science fiction tale about a mental patient and the nurse sent to look after him. The nut screeches on about four-armed invaders from the core of the earth, never knowing his protector has been sent up to silence him. The best thing about these reprints, of course, is the vintage art and Bill Everett does not disappoint with his bug-eyed doctors and four-armed babes.

For the first time ever (exclaims Roy Thomas in this issue's editorial), Marvel looked outside its own titles to cherry-pick "Sword of Dragonus," a sword and sorcery tale that appeared in a 1970 one-shot fanzine called *Phase*. I must admit to being astonished at the roll call of *Phase*'s contributors: Dan Adkins, Berni(e) Wrightson, Murphy Anderson, Ken Barr, Rich Buckler, Marv Wolfman, Gray Morrow, and "Dragonus" artist/ writer Frank Brunner. Of course, in those early days of fandom, it wasn't unheard of to find a new Jack Kirby illo on the cover of *Rocket's Blast* but a cursory scan of *Phase* shows why the starving artists contributed for nothing but comp copies: it was a testing ground that provided a portfolio for the big guys to check out your stuff. No need to hop a plane to Manhattan when The Rascally One was scouring the fan press for new talent. "Dragonus" is an unremarkable Conan knock-off with primitive but stylish art by Frank Brunner. Just a little more refinement and this guy would be ready for the big leagues.

Gerry Conway adapts Thomas M. (as opposed to the "young" Thomas A. that Roy trumpets on the editorial page) Disch's creepy crawly masterpiece, "The Roaches," a short story about a slightly-off young woman, Marcia, who finds she can control cockroaches. The pests of the title, we find, may not be the little bugs but rather the larger humanoid insects that live in the apartments around Marcia. Before anyone shouts out "Hey, haven't I seen that before?" I'll remind you that "The Roaches" actually predates **Ratman's Notebooks** (*Willard*) by four years. This remains one of the highlights (for me) of the B&W era but I'd caution Gerry that using the same last line (or a variation of such) in two stories in the same issue can raise red flags.

Now if we could just get rid of the worthless pun-filled text pieces. Isabella's review of Denis Gifford's Karloff "bio" is informative (and would read much more scholarly minus the afore-mentioned puns) but Pasko's "examination" of the three Karloff/Universal Frankenstein films reads like a mini-*Famous Monsters* filmbook. There are no critical comments to speak of but then, considering Pasko sums up *Son of Frankenstein* with a dismissive "Son loses something of its predecessor's moody atmosphere . . . ", I'd say we were spared an article full of ludicrous statements. This Universal fan wonders if Pasko had even seen *Son*, a dark, noirish classic dripping with atmosphere and gothic menace. The lack of real journalism in these non-fiction pieces doesn't bode well for a revisit of a childhood fave, *Monsters of the Movies*, Marvel's inevitable answer to *Famous Monsters of Filmland*.

Monsters Unleashed #3 (November 1973)
Cover by Neal Adams

"Man-Thing!"
Story by Roy Thomas and Gerry Conway
Art by Gray Morrow
(reprinted from *Savage Tales* #1, May 1971)

"The Cyclops"
Story by Stan Lee
Art by Jack Davis
(reprinted from *Journey Into Unknown Worlds* #50, October 1956)

"Frankenstein: AK (After Karloff)"
Non-Fiction by Martin Pasko

"The Death-Dealing Mannikin"
Story by Kit Pearson and Tony Isabella
Art by Win Mortimer

"Contact!"
Story and Art by Tom Sutton
(reprinted from *Tower of Shadows* #6, July 1970)

"Swamp Girl"
Story Uncredited
Art by Vic Carrabotta
(reprinted from *Mystic* #19, April 1953)

"Preview: The Son of Satan"
Text by Carla Joseph

"The Cold of the Uncaring Moon"
Story by Steve Skeates
Art by George Tuska and Klaus Janson

"Birthright!"
Story by Roy Thomas
Art by Gil Kane and Crusty Bunkers

For a number of reasons, this third issue of *Monsters Unleashed*, a title I loved to death as a wee lad, is one gigantic disappointment. Now, I don't remember being all that disappointed with the finished product fifty years ago, but then I really liked *Charlie's Angels* too and that just doesn't hold up these days either, does it? The Frankenstein Monster story promised on the cover doesn't show due to the death of Syd Shores. Roy Thomas lets us know on the debut letters page that the story will be finished and pop up in *MU* #5. The Son of Satan, also blurbed on the cover, turns out to be a text piece, no more than a glorified advertisement for Marvel's latest horror hero.

The reprints are a sorry bunch (do we really need another rerun of Man-Thing's origin?), taking up 22 pages, and the film history lesson is another of the ilk that makes you think Pasko read a whole bunch of *Famous Monsters* back issues to research his thesis. So what does that leave us? Three "original" stories.

In "The Death-Dealing Mannikin," Lucio, a gypsy's son who wears belted Levi's despite living in 1935 Austria, has had enough of the brutal treatment he and his family have suffered at the hands of Baron Krutze. Lucio seeks out the help of a witch, who transfers the man's soul into a clay figure and gives it the gift of movement. The dummy begins its campaign of revenge. Win Mortimer's art is abysmal, lacking anything resembling style or drama. Which is apt for the story, an unoriginal "blending" of Robert Bloch's "The Mannikin" and *The Golem*. Bottom of the barrel stuff.

But wait, there's more! "Cold of the Uncaring Moon" offers up a typical werewolf tale (tail?) with a nice twist ending but suffers, fatally, from Tuska-itis. Effectively served up as George's test run for his upcoming stint on the Man-Wolf series in *Creatures on the Loose*, it's obvious quite early that the only criteria Roy was looking for was that Tuska drew a better werewolf than Roy did. Rascally's the big-shot editor, not me, but I wouldn't have put this guy in charge of any horror title. There's nothing even remotely frightening about Tuska's lycanthrope. At least he didn't draw the thing with buckteeth. That first panel on page 52 is a Frazetta steal. Tsk, tsk, Tuska!

After the "Lastwar," two very well-developed specimens named Galt and Ayn frolic through the "lost Valley" and conquer all sorts of dreadful monsters before their handler, a robot, finds them and returns them to the breeding plant where they were born. "Birthright" isn't written by Robert E. Howard but most of it sure reads like it. What it resembles even more is the type of story Gil Kane was selling to DC's *House of Mystery* and *House of Secrets* in the late 60s and early 70s, pseudo-Sword and Sorcery. Overall, an extremely lackluster installment of *MU*. Let's put it in the rear view and hope for better next time!

Monsters Unleashed #4 (January 1974)
Cover by Pujolar

"The Classic Monster!"
Story by Gary Friedrich
Art by John Buscema, Syd Shores, and Win Mortimer

"The Hands!"
Story by Stan Lee
Art by Gene Colan
(reprinted from *Adventures Into Terror* #14, Winter 1952)

"Our Martian Heritage"
Non-Fiction by Chris Claremont

"Web of Hate"
Story by Tony Isabella
Art by Dave Cockrum

"A Monster Reborn"
Story by Steve Gerber
Art by Pablo Marcos

"The Monster Master"
Book review by Tony Isabella

"The Killers"
Story Uncredited
Art by Bernie Krigstein
(reprinted from *Adventures Into Weird Worlds* #10, September 1952)

"To Love, Honor, Cherish . . . 'Til Death!"
Story by Chris Claremont
Art by Don Perlin

"In Memorium (*sic*): Lon Chaney, Jr."

A nice Wolfman-inspired Frank Brunner painting graces the cover of the 4th Unleashing of the Monsters (*which was later used — most likely without permission — on a Norwegian edition of Richard Matheson's I Am Legend — ed.*). The insides are another matter altogether. Gary Friedrich continues to undo all the good he did with the color Frankenstein title with the latest installment of Frankenstein 1973. After the calamity at the carnival which left his girl in the hospital, Dr. Derek McDowell (the world's youngest neurosurgeon) appeals to the local gendarmes to allow him to take possession of the Frankenstein Monster. After a few greenbacks have passed into the right hands, Derek brings the Monster back to his laboratory to attempt a resuscitation. There to help him is Vulture dead-ringer, Dr. Wallach. The older man at first attempts to dissuade his colleague's perverted experiments but eventually goes along with the scheme.

The creature is resurrected and all that remains is to replace its criminal brain with that of a fresh, intelligent mind. For some reason (the influence of the 1970s, perhaps?) Derek decides the best choice would be a soft-core porn photographer. Alas, that idea ends in murder and a damaged brain when the monster goes berserk (or in the words of Derek McDowell: "Damn! He smashed the dude's skull!"). Back at the lab, a lightbulb goes on over Derek's head and he steals the brain of his partner, Dr. Wallach. Demonstrating that no good deed goes unpunished, the monster/Wallach awakens and throttles Derek, all the while laying out his plans for world domination.

We waited two issues for this bilge? John Buscema's art is hidden under an ugly second skin of Syd Shores/Win Mortimer ink. Shores had died while working on this installment and Mortimer had to step in and finish it. Everything is wrong with this plot, from the with-it hippie brain surgeon who spouts "Dude!" to the wasted monster, now merely a secondary character. The final pages, in particular, have a slapdash look to them, as if they were headed to Skywald rather than Marvel.

Speaking of Skywald, another publisher (like Warren and Eerie) that Marvel was attempting to overtake in the B&W race, it's interesting to note that Tom Sutton's Frankenstein series had been running in various Skywald titles (*Nightmare*, *Psycho*, and *Scream*) since 1970 and took the exact premise that Friedrich would employ. The initial chapters were a direct sequel to the Shelley novel and later installments found a resurrected monster in the present day. "Frankenstein 1973" appeared in *Nightmare* #13 four months after the appearance of *MU* #4 (ironically, an

appreciation of Syd Shores appeared in that same issue of *Nightmare*). At a very early age, I discovered it was much more fun to read *about* Skywald magazines than to crack one open, so I can't give the audience a learned opinion as to the merits of Skywald's Frankenstein versus Marvel's but, based on "The Classic Monster," we'll call it a draw.

Marvel, unable to license John Carter, turned to Edwin L. Arnold's *Lieut. Gullivar Jones: His Vacation* (1905), which according to Edgar Rice Burroughs biographer Richard A. Lupoff, inspired the Barsoom stories. (George Lucas also admits Jones as a *Star Wars* inspiration.) Their loose adaptation of his sword-and-planet adventures in *Creatures on the Loose* #16-21 resumed in *Monsters Unleashed* #4, where Lupoff's rediscovery of the novel, and Marvel's search for an "interplanetary s-f" Conan-style character, are rehashed.

Tony Isabella's "Web of Hate" begins with Gullivar, native wing-man Chak, and Princess of Mars Heru — last seen slaughtering warlord Ar-Hap's army with the wing-men — wandering the wilderness to reach Heru's city, Seth. Unable to return to Earth, Gullivar hopes "*to rediscover the ancient Martian science that brought [him] to the Red Planet.*" But with Mars in the "*hands* of *monsters* and *barbarians* . . . *and ruled by* *superstition*," it first "means bucking Ar-Hap's barbarians *and the* *Technics Guild*."

While they are encamped, a Noltoi hears Heru's song and is instantly enchanted. Gullivar and Chak cannot stop the creature, whom Gully fails to recognize as more human than spider, from hypnotizing and webbing Heru. The Noltoi tells Heru telepathically that she is a mutant outcast from her people, but despite Heru's efforts, an overprotective Gullivar slays "*the lonely creature [who] sought [them] out, not as* **prey** . . . *but as* **companions**." Her dying eyes offer forgiveness; Heru weeps; and Gullivar "*pray[s] to a God . . . much* **kinder** *than those on Mars . . . that . . . next time . . . [he]* **would** *be wiser*."

In *MU* #8, editor Isabella admits that the COTL series "*Bombed*," yet per *MU* #4's contents page: "By popular demand! *Gullivar Jones, Warrior of Mars* returns!" While Marvel also claimed in *COTL* #22 that "The ten-page length was a hampering factor," his return is only eleven, including Dave Cockrum's two-page COTL recap (echoing the Silver Surfer-ish image from #16 of Gully surfing a shining nimbus). Per the Bullpen, "Dave figures it's the closest thing to John Carter he'll ever get to draw," but he'd get his chance on Marvel's own Carter title.

Isabella — "one of Gully's biggest fans" — surprisingly turns from swashbuckling adventure to quasi-Greek tragedy with his uncharacteristic finale. Gullivar's continued hand-wringing over his Vietnam War service becomes overbearing, but at least this time the tone matches the story's tragic payoff. A satisfied "Gullyphile" writes in *MU* #8 that "The b&w format is perfect for Gullivar Jones," the absence of vibrant color fitting the more somber mood.

Sara Conroy works in the D.A.'s office but her husband is the chief suspect in the Hanling murders, a series of vicious knifings that has New York paralyzed with fear. Trying to prove to her boss her job comes first, she searches for her husband. When she finds him, she discovers the killer is not her husband but her boss. Luckily, her husband, Eric, who happens to be a werewolf, is in the neighborhood to save her but, sadly, dies in her arms. At story's

end, we're left hoping Sara can cope with her promotion to D.A. but confident in the knowledge that her butcher's bill won't be so high from here on out. "To Love, Honor, Cherish . . . 'Til Death" is one really bad by-the-numbers potboiler capped with a laughable reveal and expository. Inexplicably, Roy Thomas must have looked upon Don Perlin's rendition of a werewolf and thought, "Right, here's the perfect runner-up for Ploog" as Perlin would take over *Werewolf By Night* three months later. That reign of terror would limp along right up until the title's final, dreadful issue.

Our reprints this issue are a sad pair. The first, "The Hands," is a one-page joke drawn out to five about a man born with claw hands who desperately wants to be normal. He takes on a life of crime to achieve his end goal. It looks as though Gene Colan merely traced a batch of movie stills for his panels and the only moment of entertainment derived from this pre-coder is the sight of a man with lobster claws holding a pistol. "The Killers" has better art (by EC stalwart Bernie Krigstein) but is literally unreadable as the pages are presented out of order. When read in its intended incarnation, the pre-coder actually presents a novel concept for a 1950s horror story: there's a food chain for everything, including mankind.

The saving grace of the issue is Steve Gerber's reimagining of the Golem legend, "A Monster Reborn." Intelligently written (in particular, the rabbi's soul-searching dialogue), nicely penciled, and topped off with a certifiable twist ending, this is easily the best story this magazine has run in its initial four issues. Gerber's deeply moving script is completely out of place in a magazine populated by neurosurgeons with tie-dyed t-shirts who spout Kerouac-inspired exclamations and lawyers married to their job more than their werewolf husbands. Ironically, as the letters page reveals, the story was cooked up with Marv Wolfman "over lunch" when it was discovered the issue was five pages short in content. It's also revealed in the letters page that Frank Brunner's cover painting was initially set to run on the aborted third issue of *The Haunt of Horror* digest.

Monsters Unleashed #5 (April 1974)
Cover by Bob Larkin

"All the Faces of Fear!"
Story by Tony Isabella
Art by Vicente Alcazar

"The Golden Voyage of Sinbad"
Review by Gerry Conway

"The Dark Passage"
Story Uncredited
Art by Ogden Whitney
(reprinted from *Adventure Into Terror* #10, June 1952)

"Glenn Strange, Frankenstein Monster of Dodge City"
Obituary by Don Glut

"Demon of Slaughter Mansion"
Story by Don McGregor
Art by Juan Boix

"Monsters in the Media"
Text by Carla Joseph

"Werewolf Tale to End All Werewolf Tales!"
Story Uncredited
Art by Paul Hodge
(reprinted from *Journey Into Unknown Worlds* #29, July 1954)

"Once a Monster . . . !"
Story by Gary Friedrich
Art by John Buscema and Win Mortimer

First of all, is it just me or does it look as though the unusually large Man-Thing on the cover is feeding Ellie May Clampett to that alligator rather than saving her? "Right, open up, here ya go!"

"All the Faces of Fear" is a sequel, of sorts, to the very first Man-Thing adventure back in *Savage Tales* #1 (and reprinted at least sixty times since then) as Ellen Brandt, the beauty who betrayed Ted Sallis and paid the piper in the form of a burnt and mangled kisser, returns to the swamp to face her fears and put an end to the Man-Thing. Once she confronts the big muck monster though, she loses all her fears and faces the truth that her problems are all a result of her own actions. Not too bad, this one, although it's got a few lapses in reason (would the equipment of A.I.M. still be cluttering up the swamps if it was worth a fortune?) and logic. Vicente Alcazar does a nice job drumming up atmosphere and his unbandaged Ellen is a babe to behold. Isabella lays down a few hints at what's to come and I'll be tuning in to see if those threads become anything of substance. It is nice to find something of Isabella's I don't have to stomp on.

Coming upon the form of Laura Devlon in the forest, reporter Daniel Cambridge carries the girl back to her parents' home deep in the forest. There he learns about a deadly family secret and becomes swept up in a centuries-old curse. Will the Devlon family be wiped off the face of the earth by "The Demon of Slaughter Mansion" or will love save the day? Promised twice before and twice before postponed, this could very well be the worst crap Marvel ever published in its black and white history. From its pretentious dialogue (" . . . *the hatred in its eyes were like those of an animal whose leg is maimed in a trap, glaring at the enemy who set it. Even though you're here . . . we're still . . . the self-imprisoned!*") to its awful art (every panel posed, not one bit natural) and a letterer who could have benefited greatly from spell check (" . . . *as if he cannot* **bare** *to be alone!*"), "Demon" misfires on all cylinders. At one point, Cambridge comments that the proceedings are "beginning to take on overtones of a gothic novel." I'd agree. It's a rotten, nonsensical, pulpy gothic, possibly inspired by the type DC was running in *Dark Mansion of Forbidden Love* and *The Sinister House of Secret Love*. Well, why not? I think, by this time, the tentacles of Marvel were reaching out in just about every direction. By the way, pages 8 and 9 were originally printed out of order but the climax may actually make more sense if you read them out of sequence. Can't hurt.

"Once a Monster . . . " is another chapter in the never-ending saga that should have been titled "The Brains of Frankenstein." Luckily, the crazed scientist who finds his grey matter in the head of the Monster had just completed work on a "molecular transposer," a gizmo that allows him to do brain surgery on himself! This comes in handy when he finds a hunky body to shift minds into. In an obvious "nod" to *The Fly*, catastrophe strikes when a stray mouse shimmies up the receiving body and gets its brain zapped into the Monster. That leaves the scientist in the body of the mouse and the reader hoping Gary Friedrich's problems on this B&W series don't translate over to the generally well-written color series. Win Mortimer is not doing Big John any favors.

"The Dark Passage" is yet another riff on "An Occurrence at Owl Creek Bridge," but "Werewolf Tale to End All Werewolf Tales" is a charming bit of nonsense about a couple who spend their honeymoon in a cabin set in what their French servant calls "Loup Garou country." Our uncredited documenter tries to throw suspicion on Henri the servant but I knew better. The "reveal" isn't all that startling but it will bring a smile to even the most jaded of horror fans.

Gerry Conway gives us the skinny on Ray Harryhausen's then-current Sinbad flick while dropping a little behind-the-scenes news on the forthcoming adaptation of the flick (in *Worlds Unknown* 7 and 8). There's nothing here resembling critical journalism but, when dealing with a Harryhausen movie, that seems to be the norm. Out comes the "Gosh wow, I grew up on Harryhausen!" If you wanted objectivity, you'd have to pick up *Photon* or *Cinefantastique* in those days, not something penned by Marvel comic book writers. End rant.

While I enjoyed Glenn Strange's performances as the Monster in a couple of Universal monster rallies, I find it odd that more space was afforded his death than that of Lon Chaney, Jr. a couple months prior. Carla Joseph continues to monkey with her news column (now with the more descriptive title of "Monsters in the Media"), including differentiating between "Recent Releases" (*The Boy Who Cried Werewolf*, etc.) and "Oldies and Goldies" (*Night of the Living Dead*, etc.). While there's nothing approaching ground-breaking journalism, Joseph's little tidbits and micro-reviews are breezy reading and will have to do until *Monsters of the Movies* makes its debut in August.

Monsters Unleashed #6 (June 1974)
Cover by Boris Vallejo

"Always a Monster"
Story by Doug Moench
Art by Val Mayerik

"Monsters in the Media"
News by Carla Joseph

"The Strange Children"
Story Uncredited
Art by Sam Kweskin
(Reprinted from *Adventures into Terror* #19, May 1953)

"The Dinosaur Dictionary"
A review by Chris Claremont

"Darkflame!"
Story by Gerry Conway
Art by Carlo Freixas

"Panic by Moonlight"
Text by Gerry Conway
Art by Mike Ploog

"The Maggots!"
Story by Paul S. Newman
Art by Hy Rosen
(Reprinted from *Adventures into Terror* #19, May 1953)

"The Scrimshaw Serpent"
Story by Doug Moench
Art by Alfonso Font

This is complicated, so pay attention. I won't repeat myself. In our last thrilling episode of Frankenstein 1974, the Monster had had his brain replaced with that of a mouse (for the sake of my own narrative, let's refer to him as Fluffy), Dr. Wallach the mad scientist who performed the experiment (with his brilliant "Transposer") switched brains with a trapeze artist, and assistant Derek McDowell's brain now resides in a moldering, shambling corpse. Said assistant seems to be the least happiest of the quartet (with Fluffy enjoying every minute of his newfound height -- he's hanging around in alleyways squishing brother and sister mice), and so heads out in search of the monster (he mistakenly thinks the doctor's brain is in the monster's body). When Derek gets back to the lab, he finds the trapeze artist's body and makes a switch so that he can wander the city unmolested (I would have sworn the trapeze guy was killed last issue but if you think I'm going back to check . . .). He grabs a rifle and finally catches up to our patchwork hero, shooting him with tranquilizer darts. Once back in the lab (here's the confusing part) he "transposes" the mouse's brain out of the monster and sends the monster's original brain back into his body. This displeases Frankenstein's monster and he throws Derek against the wall, smashing his skull. As the brute is leaving the lab, the trapeze artist (now in the decaying corpse) awakens and, recognizing the murderer of his wife (which happened last issue), scolds him. The last panels reveal that someone else is watching the proceeding from afar, someone who claims to have orchestrated the entire drama. I've left so much out but, trust me, you don't want to know more. It would only spoil your enjoyment of this, the ***Bob & Carol & Ted & Alice*** of comic book brain transplants. If I was having a hard time keeping characters straight, how the hell was Moench doing it while he was creating the entire opera? I have no idea if Doug meant this to be chuckled at or if he was dead serious. You couldn't tell from the pretentious writing that opens the saga:

A diffuse curtain of languid fog shrouds the bleak stage: the squalid bank of the East River. Major prop: a bottle of dismal memories, from which long gulps of forgetfulness are taken by the supporting character: a seedy derelict with a one-way ticket to misery, his only possessions being wasted years and shattered dreams. The action: slow, sinister. A groping hand, bloated and corroded with decay, breaks the river's surface at the center of sad ripples . . . an ooze-crusted, stench-reeking hand of withering pestilence which belongs to the star: Derek McDowell.

Who does Moench think he is? Rod Serling? It goes on like that for a bit, the analogy to film, and then is just dropped randomly a couple pages in. There's a

whole lot here to laugh at besides the self-loving prose. That ill-fated drunk at the beginning of the story, the one who watches McDowell's festering, pus-filled reanimated corpse rise from the river is the same derelict who watched Derek's clean-shaven, pimple-free body floating last issue! McDowell's corpse shouldn't really be moldering and rotting since, ostensibly, it had just been dumped in the river a few hours before. I'll buy the bloated part (even though Mayerik doesn't present the corpse as such) but not corroded and pestilent. And why the hell does the corpse rise in the first place? Should I be patient and all will be revealed next issue? When McDowell "transposes" the brain of the mouse from the monster, it's a really tiny brain. I assumed that it was the memories of the donors that were switched, not the actual grey matter itself. That panel of the pea-brain is a riot. After dozens of brain switches and pounded heads, we're right back to the beginning of the series, with nothing having been accomplished but wasted pages. I love Val Mayerik's art and it's a no-brainer (pun intended) that he should handle chores on this and the four-color *The Frankenstein Monster* but there's a danger that his work on this and "The Living Mummy" could become formulaic.

Steve Skeates's massively enjoyable and massively kitschy "The Mummy Walks" series in Warren's *Eerie* had pretty much the same storyline as this. Only time will tell if Frankenstein 1974 will climb such lofty heights.

The other two new stories this issue are both readable. "Darkflame!" is a genuine throwback to the Lee/Kirby giant monster days marred only by amateurish art by newcomer Carlo Freixas. There's nothing new to Gerry Conway's tale of a giant winged monster that rises from an erupted volcano but, sometimes, you don't need new. The same goes for "The Scrimshaw Serpent," a tale of revenge and sculpted demons, with an intelligent script by Doug Moench and sub-par art by another rookie, Alfonso Font. Both from Spain, Font and Freixas were riding in on the wave of foreign talent that invaded American comics in the early 1970s. This was Font's second, and final, contribution to the B&Ws (his first being "Shadow in the City of Light!" back in *Dracula Lives* #3) and Freixas would be back in *MU* #7.

The reprints, both from *Adventures into Terror* #19, showcase nasty little buggers. A curse on a small village turns all the children into cockroaches ("The Strange Children") and a scientist discovers that "The Maggots" are impatient little critters and don't necessarily wait until their host is dead to start munching. Neither story is worth reprinting. How hard would it have been to scour the pages of Atlas' horror titles to find quality stories?

Monsters Unleashed #7 (August 1974)
Cover by Richard Hescox

"A Tale of Two Monsters!"
Story by Doug Moench
Art by Val Mayerik

"The Monster in the Mist"
Story Uncredited
Art by Al Williamson
(reprinted from *Astonishing* #60, April 1957)

"The Frankenstein Legend"
Book Review by Alan Gold

"Bleeding Stones"
Story by Doug Moench
Art by Vicente Alcazar

"Madness Under a Midsummer Moon"
Text Story by Gerry Conway

"Blind Man's Bluff"
Story by Gerry Conway
Art by Carlos Freixas

"Monsters in the Media"
News by Carla Joseph

The Frankenstein Monster sits and listens patiently as the trapeze artist tells him how he came to be just another unlucky stiff stuck in the body of . . . an unlucky stiff. The mysterious man behind the curtain who has been planning all the mayhem (and controls the body the trapeze artist is trapped in) orders the corpse to shamble to his residence and bring the big guy with him. Once they step inside the eerie mansion, trapeze guy collapses, dead, and the floor opens, sending the Monster down a slide into the clutches of the controller, a twisted freak who lords over a horde of nasty subjects. This series continues to spiral down into a meandering time-waster. Some time-wasters are good; not this one. More and more, I get the feeling that Doug Moench never had a clue where to take this strip so he'd just get by from issue to issue. In "A Tale of Two Monsters," Doug stops the "action" for a detailed and unremarkable flashback/origin of a character he kills off three pages later. Other than that, absolutely nothing happens. We finally get to see who's behind the "orchestration" of our little drama and it's just another freak. This series has cornered the market on freaks; they've become the go-to plot device for Moench.

"Bleeding Stones" may have been Doug Moench's offer to fans who'd written him off because of the Frankenstein debacle. A tyrannical general demands a priest pay taxes on his church or the holy house will be brought down. Meanwhile, we discover that the architect who sculpted the gargoyles for the church stashed a fortune in gold coins inside the statues. When the architect badly beats the priest, the gargoyles come to life and exact revenge. A strange story this one in that Moench introduces who we assume to be the "bad guy" (the general) and then writes him out of the script in order to make way for a completely different villain. The "gargoyles come to life" theme has been done much better (perhaps the best

icons, this one and **The Dracula Book**. Neither one is above criticism (but I can't find anything to complain about either, sorry) but Gold seems to hate the book because it's full of plot summaries and other real icky stuff. How can anyone take seriously a critic who exclaims (in crayon, no doubt) "Hammer had a chance for fresh thinking but didn't accept the challenge. Their Frankenstein films add nothing to "The Legend." They created no permanent image to compete with Universal's, so this chapter, like the one before it (on the equally maligned Universal Frankenstein films) and those that follow, would probably have been better as a footnote or an appendix somewhere." In the end, Gold could have saved three pages of text and simply stated "I din't like it cuz I dunt like Frankastyn!"

Monsters Unleashed #8 (October 1974)
Cover by Earl Norem

"Fever in the Freak House"
Story by Doug Moench
Art by Val Mayerik

"Man-Thing: Several Meaningless Deaths"
Text Story by Steve Gerber
Art by Pat Broderick and Al Milgrom

"Swamp Stars of the Silver Screen"
Text by Don Glut

"One Hungers"
(reprinted from *Tower of Shadows* #2, November 1969)

"A Martian Genesis"
Story by Tony Isabella and Doug Moench
Art by George Perez, Duffy Vohland, and Rich Buckler

In a trend we'll see more of in the next few months, Tony Isabella rhapsodizes in his editorial column about all the wonderful changes that will be taking effect in the next few months. Lots of new series characters and heaps of great stuff. "The Tiger" won't see most of these changes implemented (and most will be forgotten as early as next issue's editorial) as he's basically a "dead editor walking" and won't last past #9. All the wonderfulness Tony promises surely could not have begun this issue as what we get here is two new stories, a reprint, and a boatload of text. Editor Isabella claims that "This is Your Magazine!" If so, I think I'll look for another one.

Having witnessed the psychic murder

example being Jack Oleck's "The House of Gargoyles" from *House of Mystery* #175, August 1968) than this but it's still a fun time. Not so much fun is "Blind Man's Bluff," a *Curse of the Demon* knock-off that adds nothing to the "white man pillages ancient temple and then pays the price" cliche. "Blind Man's Bluff" seems almost a sequel to last issue's "Darkflame!" (also by the Conway/Freixas team) in that Conway patches together bits of old horror movies in a script and then hands it over to Carlos Freixas, who obviously has a very limited imagination when it comes to monsters. "Bluff"'s Ch'Manu has the same overall look as the Godzilla rip-off known as "Darkflame!" The title, by the way, gives away the lame twist.

Rounding out the issue is "The Monster in the Mist," a reprint featuring sharp art by Al Williamson and a laugh-out-loud expository; Carla Joseph's usual mumblings about genre cinema (which, more and more, look as though they were lifted from *Famous Monsters*); and a Werewolf by Night text story with some nice spot illos by Pat Broderick and Klaus Janson.

Special mention must be made of the idiotic review of a very good book, Don Glut's **The Frankenstein Legend**. Glut wrote two indispensable books on horror of his only friend, The Frankenstein Monster is, shall we say, a little peeved at his new nemesis, The Master, a really ugly guy who commands a horde of experiments-gone-wrong in a dank and smelly dungeon. The Master tries valiantly to bring The Monster on board his revival of ugliness but the big guy ain't having any so there's a "Fever in the Freak House!" The Master has an ace up his sleeve in the guise of a gas-filled rocket launcher which he uses to halt The Monster's rampage. With the beast out of the way, the freak boss orders his squadron to converge upon Julia Winters, a fine specimen and, it appears, a babe he used to stalk.

Once Julia is shackled and helpless, The Master surprises everyone by pulling off his gruesome face and revealing that, under it all, he's actually a pretty boy. This drives his congregation nuts (they so wanted him to be one of them!) and they rip the former Master to pieces. The disagreement gives The Frankenstein Monster a chance to break free of his chains, bust Julia out, and escape the Freak House just before the walls come tumbling down. Outside, a patrol car rolls up and another bad day begins for our patchwork hero. As I've noted before regarding this series, I believe neither Gary Friedrich nor Doug Moench had any idea where to take this series nor what to do with this character. I don't blame them. Aside from teaming him with Dracula or Werewolf by Night, what do you do to keep The Monster interesting? Not this mess.

The splash reads that Frankenstein's Monster is "wrenching in horror, utter dismay slicing his consciousness, livid realization laying devastating waste to the newly-found succor of companionship" but you could have fooled me. His expression looks more like boredom, as if he was forced to read the script he was trapped in (or, worse, Tony's editorial). Doug may have been reading Len Wein's *Swamp Thing* at the time and thought freaks was the way to go. I know this hook, the real ugly guy who turns out to be dashing under the mask, has been played before, I just can't remember where. A Special No-No Prize to the first reader who reminds

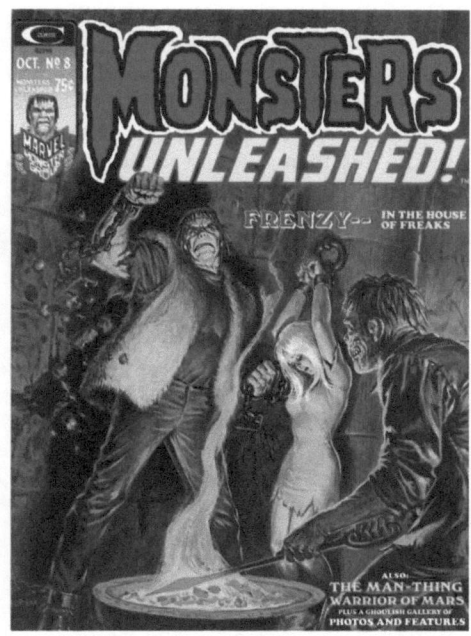

me where I may have seen it.

Gullivar Jones returns in "A Martian Genesis!" The exiles defeat a hideous creature near Seth, but the Hither-People, barred by the guild, are encamped outside; disgusted with their attempts to make her a peace offering to Ar-Hap, Heru threatens her "race of *cringing cowards!*" at knifepoint, and they part to let the trio enter. The "Sacred City of *Technological Redemption* and *Scientific Salvation*" is a ghost town: tripping an alarm, they are swarmed by winged slugs, holding their own until guild members sleep-gas and take them to the Hall of Science, condemned for trespassing. The cloaked guild — its faith that "this world's *only hope* lies in *science*" unshaken, and its "perfect beings" hybrid monsters — judges humankind *"undeserving of life!"*

One uncowls, revealing radiation's effects upon them, unlike their "superior" species, e.g., the *"Firstborn!* . . . a blasphemous entity belched up on a *geyser of flame* rooted in the pits of *hell* . . . " As Gullivar breaks his chains, frees his friends, and topples the tentacled beast, the scientists despair at its death; he upbraids them for building "tinker-toy *mockeries* of life!" instead of "search[ing] for ways to *save* the *dying races*," and tongue-lashes them New York-style: "Bozos," "jerks!," "crybabies." Gully despairs that "the *last scientists on Mars*" can return him to Earth, but per Heru, hope lies in "[t]he *real* knowledge of this city . . . in *books*. If we can *find* them, we can *use* those books the way they *should* be."

Isabella and Doug Moench refer to "*secur[ing] an audience with the Wonderful Wizard of Oz*," but these genetic engineers behind the curtain are worse than L. Frank Baum's buffoon; this cautionary tale about playing God suits Arnold's Edwardian age or the Romantic era of Frankenstein and Moreau. They recall Charlton Heston's foes from **Beneath the Planet of the Apes** or **The Omega Man**, while previously, Gullivar resembled Buster Crabbe. George Pérez, Duffy Vohland, and Rich Buckler seem to anticipate another Flash Gordon — Sam J. Jones — worst of all Gully's newly flowing mane.

Gullivar reaches his goal, but never clicks his heels together to go home; will they roam the Dying Planet till their dying days? Marvel's conclusion diverges wildly from Arnold's, which foreshadowed *Apollo 11* in grand jingoistic style: "'*All ownerless, and with so much treasure hidden hereabout! Why, I shall annex it to my country . . . ' I whipped out my sword, and in default of a star-spangled banner to plant on the newly-acquired territory, traced in gigantic letters on the snow-crust — U.S.A.*"

There's also a prose Man-Thing story, a look at filmic swamp monsters, and a reprint whose ink is barely dry from its original appearance. Down, down, down slides a title that could have been so much more.

Monsters Unleashed # 9 (December 1974)
Cover by Earl Norem

"The Conscience of the Creature"
Story by Doug Moench
Art by Val Mayerik

"The Jewel That Snarled at Slight Greed"
Story by Doug Moench
Art by Don Perlin

"Several Meaningless Deaths (Part Two)"
Text Story by Steve Gerber

"Snowbird in Hell"
Story by Chris Claremont
Art by Yong Montano

After saving Julie Winters from

the parade of freaks (last issue), The Frankenstein Monster carries her unconscious form out of the hell house and into the pointed guns of the law. After the monster cuts a swath through the officers, the monster carries Julie into the city to find her home. Before they get there, they must traverse a seemingly unending series of obstacles, including released zoo animals and another squad of cops. Through all this, all the monster wants is a bit of love. When Julie awakens and sees her savior, she gives him just the opposite, punctuated with a stone to the monster's kisser. Our hero is left pondering what is and what never shall be. As I've mentioned ad nauseam (I should just rerun my comments from the last several issues), the wheels are stuck in the mud and a'spinnin', the same fate that befell most of the other short-run horror series of the mid-1970s (the obvious exceptions being *Man-Thing* and *Tomb of Dracula*). Frankenstein 1974 is still searching for that elusive hook to hang a decent plot line on. Nothing happens in "The Conscience of the Creature" that would resonate in further adventures and all we're stuck with is more flowery prose from Doug "The Poet" Moench. Doug reminds me of the nerdy guy in seventh grade who'd suck up to the teacher by writing variations of **The Scarlet Letter** and **Animal Farm** (*"Where gnarled tree limbs twist into a fiber of gloom and uncertainty, the monster finds solace and tranquility. Where shadows spurt from nighted despair, the monster shuffles through a fragrant landscape of hope"*). Yeesh! Val's art (especially the monster's battle with a pair of escaped tigers at the zoo) remains just as consistently creepy and atmospheric.

Much better is the fantasy tale "The Jewel that Snarled at Slight Greed" where two magical events collide: Doug finds a sense of humor and Don Perlin knocks out decent art. A troll steals the blood-jewel from a bitchy queen and pairs up with a centaur to fight a three-headed dragon released from the jewel by a sorcerer. This is the type of story Gil Kane would have illustrated for DC Comics' mystery line in the late 1960s, a perfect combo of swords, sorcery, and silliness.

The biggest letdown this issue is "Snowbird in Hell," the cover story featuring The Wendigo. Picking up four months after the events of *The Incredible Hulk* #181, "Snowbird" is yet another variation on **The Thing From Another World**, with the big white snowy fanged guy picking off members of a group stuck in a remote snow-covered church. Since bullets won't kill the beast, one of the members gets the bright idea of luring the Wendigo in and burning down the church. That doesn't go as planned and the survivors are left to the elements. The Wendigo is a very cool creation and you'd expect, in the hands of future superstar Chris Claremont, a very cool eleven pages. Hints of greatness pop out here and there (when Wendigo grabs a female parishioner and takes her out for a quick bite) but only brief glimpses. Yong Montano's Wendigo is a pretty beast (with a pretty big booty, by the way), not the savage killer portrayed in Earl Norem's fabulous cover painting; his hair is parted, his nails are clipped, and there appear to be no spaces between his teeth. Claremont's script has the right skeleton but it's not filled in with the right meat. The aforementioned scene of the Wendigo dragging a screaming Madame Valery away while the others listen helplessly is very effective but what happens next? The plan to burn the church down goes awry but the survivors don't look particularly concerned when it all goes tits up, despite the fact that they're all going to be eaten or freeze to death within a matter of hours. This was one Marvel monster I would have liked to have seen more of.

In Tony Isabella's editorial this issue (his last before Don McGregor takes over), The Tiger lets us in on the fact that "due to the unprecedented deluge of letters (he's) been receiving recently, (he's) pleased to announce that — starting next issue — *Monsters Unleashed* will be an all-series magazine." That's a practice that lasted . . . well, it actually never was initiated, ostensibly as a result of Isabella's ousting. I wonder what the "unprecedented" number of letter writers thought about their wishes being ignored? The roster of upcoming projects is mouth-watering: the introduction of new horror heroes known as The Scarecrow (a story which won't see newsprint until the final issue of the reprint title, *Dead of Night*, in August of '75) and The Manphibian (who saw his origin story shelved until *The Legion of Monsters* #1 in September 1975); a text story featuring Killraven (never happened); and new stories featuring The Golem and IT! (merciful heavens!). The only promised attraction that saw fruition was the first solo appearance of Tigra, which popped up in *MU* #10. Promises, promises.

Monsters Unleashed #10 (February 1975)
Cover by Jose Antonio Domingo

"The 11:10 to Murder"
Story by Doug Moench
Art by Val Mayerik

"Beauty's Vengeance"
Story by Doug Moench
Art by Sanho Kim

"The Serenity Stealers"
Story by Tony Isabella and Chris Claremont
Art by Tony DeZuniga

The Frankenstein Monster finds himself on "The 11:10 to Murder," a train carrying a most unexpected rider: the President of the United States. But, being this a series starring Dr. Frankenstein's favorite son, trouble can't be too far away. Also riding

and pop references that litter the landscape of a Doug Moench script. But despite the annoying inanities and exclamations (the hobo girl on her situation: "I had to choose *The Parallax View* over the re-release of *Animal Crackers!*"), it's an exciting and fun ride, a first for this series and the climax is actually poignant rather than soggy for once. But, seriously, Doug, when will you have the monster meet someone who doesn't compare their situation to a Beatles song or Bertolucci film? How about a supporting character that isn't young and culturally with-it? Mayerik's art, as usual, is stellar.

A Japanese sailor happens upon a mermaid caught on some rocks and frees her. The fishy girl is thankful but the sailor tells her that's not good enough. He wants her as his own. She tells him to go home and come back in one year, and if nothing has changed, she'll belong to him. He heads back home and waiting for him is a woman who asks if she can be his servant. He agrees, and soon she begins to have feelings for her master. For his part, he sees nothing but the image of the mermaid, ignoring the kindnesses the woman doles out to him on a daily basis. The year passes and he heads back to the sea, searching for the mermaid. She finds him and, when he tells her the new woman meant nothing to him, she tells him that is because he cannot see inner beauty and therefore is not man enough for her. She kills him and it's then revealed that the servant was the mermaid in disguise. As with his Frankenstein entry this issue, Doug Moench manages to rein in his poetic self and just let the events unfold. The twist in "Beauty's Vengeance" was not much of a surprise if you're paying attention, but the message isn't laid on thick. It's as though someone told Doug that, sometimes, all you need to do is tell a good story.

this express train is a band of armed assassins trying to make their way through Secret Service agents to the POTUS's cabin. The only thing preventing a President Rockefeller is the monster and a female hobo. The duo fight their way forward through both assassins and SSAs until they are the only two standing in front of the POTUS's cabin. When the monster tears through the door, they find nothing but a dummy and realize that the entire trip was a ruse to mask the POTUS's real trip route. The girl urges the monster to jump ship before they pull into the next station since it would be hard to explain a legendary creature and several corpses on the POTUS's train. But the train doesn't stop and, unbeknownst to the monster, an assassin hurls a bomb into the car, destroying the train and killing the monster's new friend.

A really good story is tough to find in this series and this one just manages to eke out that commendation. Of course, you must first dodge the flowery prose ("*Softly, silent snow whispers to the ground, pieces of crystal cloud brushed from sky, sighing downward, breathing promises of virginity to a landscape raped by filth and soot . . .*") and dialogue that no human being would actually speak, peppered with one-liners

Prowling the Chicago streets, Tigra sees devoted family man Richard Diaz inexplicably killed by visions of his loved ones, and a murine monster feed on his essence. She loses him, learns from Joanne that this was but the latest in a series of murders, and follows "Ratso" into a sewer tunnel after "super-stud"

Brock Hunter dies seeing himself changed into a woman. In a cavernous throne room, Aeskla passes the life-force to his mistress, Surisha, who feeds on serenity and sends Aeskla for another victim, the just-downsized Lou Edwards; Tigra battles Surisha, drawing blood and instilling fear, so that when Aeskla is summoned back, he senses her vulnerability and kills her, thus destroying both halves of their symbiotic organism.

Seven months after introducing Tigra in *Giant-Size Creatures* #1, Isabella plots her first solo story, "The Serenity Stealers," and a year later will inaugurate her short-lived four-color series in *Marvel Chillers*. This is a deliberately nasty tail — er, tale — befitting the more mature B&W line; the art by Filipino DC vet DeZuniga (1932-2012), with whose work as a penciler we are largely unacquainted, is suitably dark in every sense of the word. Claremont's script can't decide on the spelling of "Ratso's" real name (Aeskla vs. Aesklos), but helps establish the new personality of Tigra — whose changeling status makes her immune to Sushira's power — as "*a joker, a wild card tossed out of a bummer hand — the fuzzy freak from the funny animal farm . . . 'mighty warrior from out of legend . . . '*"

Monsters Unleashed #11 (April 1975)
Cover by Frank Brunner

"An Angel Felled!"
Story by Doug Moench
Art by Sonny Trinidad

"The Empire"
Story by Gerry Conway
Art by Rico Rival

"This is the Valiant One, Signing Out!"
Story by Don McGregor
Art by Billy Graham

In his final appearance before a long vacation, Gabriel, the Demon Slayer, has twin emotional peaks to climb: he's still having trouble adjusting to losing his wife, Andrea (and further adjusting to the fact that her soul has commandeered Gabriel's assistant, the lovely but mysterious Desadia), and another demon possession requires his attention. Mrs. Ramirez is delighted to find her husband in bed with her one morning but she's a bit puzzled since he died a year before. Behind the

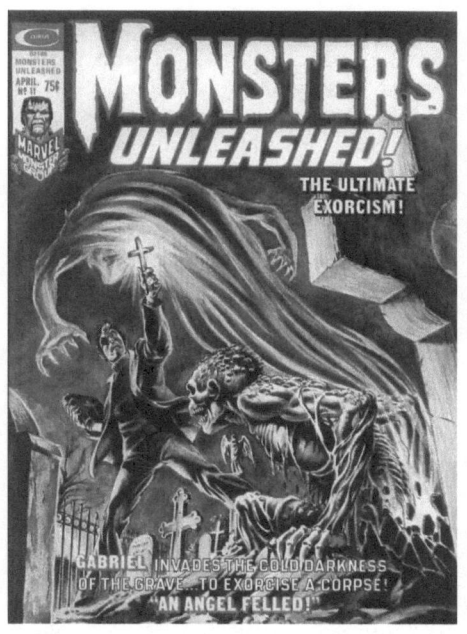

trickery is Belial, a particularly ornery demon who uses the dead man to get to Gabriel. The demon-slayer uses all of his powers to rid the world of Belial, but it takes a showdown in the graveyard before our hero can walk away a victor. Aside from the usual nods to *that* flick (the demon, at one point asks Gabriel if it's a "good day for an exorcism" and Gabriel delivers a beating to the creature when it mimes Andrea), Doug delivers a swell read, with lots of background on Gabriel's past and some insight into the intriguing concept of Desadia's inner person. It still makes me chuckle when demons hurl such PG-13 profanities as "*I do know about your God . . . I know how much he stinks! I'm saving up my spit for his bath . . .* " but, overall, this is a series that may have been getting its act together.

For decades, publishing mogul Sandor has been stepping on fragile egos (resulting in a few suicides along the way) and trampling creative rights to build "The Empire." As far as his editor, Cortman, is concerned, enough is enough. At the opening of Sandor's skyscraper, Cortman grabs hold of the microphone and tells the audience all about his boss' historic career. At the climax, he unveils a present for his boss: a giant tome titled **Publish and**

Perish which falls onto Sandor and flattens him like a pancake. At least I think it does. You can't really tell from the badly-drawn final panel if there's a giant hand attached to the book or if that's the curtain. What egomaniacal boss is going to let one of his employees go on at length about what a rotten guy he is (*and insinuating he's a murderer as well*)? This is one of those stories written by an edgy funny-book writer who wanted to show there warn't no strings on him. Of course, Gerry Conway was writing under a work-for-hire contract at the time and he may have been subtly jabbing the prez of Marvel. At any rate, it's not a very good story.

I'm going to skip the usual rote synopsis for "This is the Valiant One, Signing Out!" and just get down to the nitty-gritty. In his editorial for the final issue of *Monsters Unleashed*, Don McGregor relates how "Valiant One" finally ended up in these pages after a long, strange trip. Rejected in March 1971 at Warren (Don doesn't name names but it would have been Archie Goodwin who did the rejecting) because, Don claims, of the "National Guard element of the story." But then, happily, Don found himself editor of *MU* and deemed the story worthy for public consumption, if he do say so hisself.

If "The Empire" smacks of pretension, "Valiant One" (with its split-screen gimmickry telling two parallel stories that somehow are linked but you coulda fooled me) oozes it from every badly-drawn panel and self-important line of dialogue. I know why this was rejected by Warren, a company that published some really pretentious work by McGregor — because it was a bad story. Rather than wasting your time on this tripe, seek out the classic "The Destructive Image" (from *Creepy* #57) or "Not a Creature Was Stirring" (from *Creepy* #59) for proof that McGregor could be a very good horror writer when he wanted to be. McGregor foisting "Valiant One" on his readers is like the grocer selling that month-old bread that's gone moldy and stale. And that's as good a segue as any I've ever come up with to a wrap-up of Marvel's second black and white monster magazine. I know the talent was there but, aside from the rare highlight (remember Ralph Reese's "The Roaches" way back in #2?), this was one issue of forgettable pap after another. Good riddance.

(A *Monsters Unleashed* Annual was released in the Fall of '75, but no original content was featured.)

•••

S. Craig Zahler on . . . Five-Star Fiction

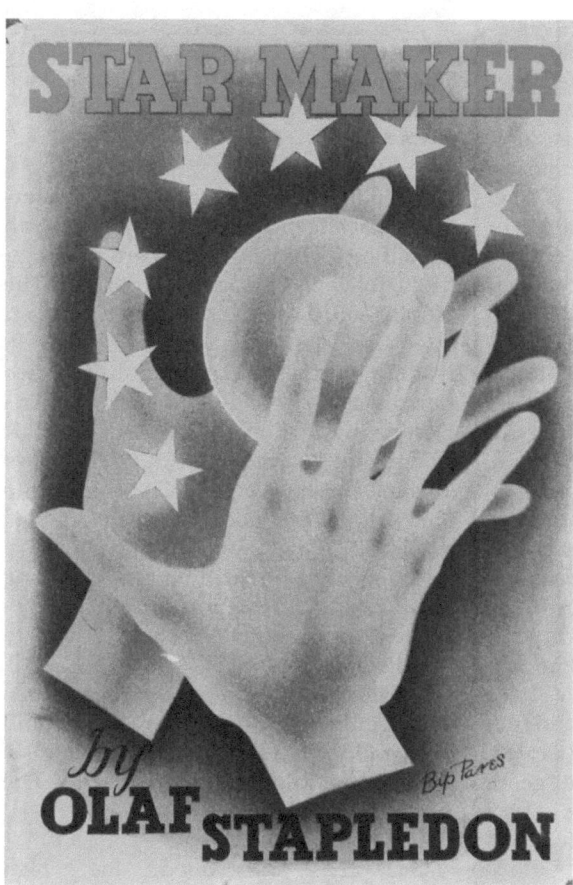

Star Maker by Olaf Stapledon
(1937)
★★★★★

    Star Maker inverts the compliment commonly given to nonfiction books: "It's so good, it reads like fiction." Olaf Stapledon's 1937 novel reads like nonfiction — cerebral, dry, and academic nonfiction sans drama, sans conflict, sans characterization, and sans humor composed of many paragraph-length sentences. And yet, the awe-inspiring cosmological, astronomical, anthropological, xenobiological, hyperdimensional, sociological, and ontological ideas contained in **Star Maker** are staggering and myriad. More than 95% of the events in this book are told rather than shown, but the vision and originality here far exceeds any I've found in so-called Golden Age sci-fi stories of the 1940s (as do my favorite Stanley G. Weinbaum and Donald Wandrei tales from the

1930s). Stapledon's brilliant inventions in this book are John Coltrane's saxophone on **A Love Supreme** and Dave Mustaine's riffs on **Rust in Peace**, though unlike those artists who employ the standardized frameworks of a jazz quartet and a metal band, this author eschews most of the aspects of a traditional novel.

Stapledon's inexorable investigations illuminate alien cultures akin to mankind, alien cultures very far removed from mankind, inscrutable communal intelligences, besmirched and self-conscious astral bodies, symbiotic evolutions, metaphysical communities, and artificial planeteers. My favorite sections deal with disruptive solar events (rare moments of tension), the space "perverts," and the alien civilizations. These aren't green, one-eyed martians, but very exotic aliens: the weirdly evolved plant men are fascinating as are the symbiotic relationships between arachnoids and ichthyoids. The bizarre progenitive rites of the nautiloids are unique, and the composite avian species is brilliantly conceived. And how about a cosmos with no spatial dimensions, but only sonic ones wherein live musical notes? Each race is worthy of its own book or movie, but is just a single chapter or page in this creative cornucopia.

At one point, Stapledon mentioned the perils of a worm falling half an inch on a world with incredibly high gravity, and I could not help but think of Hal Clement's **Mission of Gravity**, the novel often credited as being the first hard sci-fi novel (and recommended by me as well). I don't know if Clement was inspired by Stapledon, but the point I'd like to make is that this idea — a lone sentence not even amongst top five best ideas in that chapter — was a fertile enough seed to grow an entire novel. And other key concepts in this book appear in **Childhood's End**, my favorite book by Arthur C. Clarke. I see connections to Robert L. Forward and (my #1 favorite sci-fi author) Greg Egan as well.

Star Maker is a distillation of the "genre of big ideas" down to just its "big ideas," and it is a vast, highly inquisitive, and mind-expanding journey.

The Children of Húrin by J.R.R. Tolkien (2007)
★★★★★

In the 1980s, I suggested more than a few times that all religious texts on planet Earth should be replaced by **The Lord of Rings**. J.R.R. Tolkien's best known epic (and **The Hobbit**) and the works of Robert E. Howard interested a twelve year-old Zahler in reading fiction and playing RPGs, two pursuits that profoundly impacted my life. Despite my fondness for Tolkien's mythic trilogy and its prequel, I found **The Two Towers** a bit of a chore when compared to the excellent first book and the emotional third part . . . and I was never able to make it through **The Simarillion** as a kid. Long have I associated this author with his well-known works and considered the door to Middle-earth closed.

I've not read Tolkien in over thirty years, and I didn't know how much I would or wouldn't enjoy the posthumously published Middle-earth novel, **The Children of Húrin**.

This book is excellent.

Once I transcended the nigh

unintelligible profusion of proper nouns that flooded the first three pages, I was transported to a deeply melancholic and incredibly rich otherworld. This novel has the mythic, fabular quality of Lord Dunsany and the heavy atmosphere of Clark Ashton Smith (my favorite fantasist), as well as the exotic names and dense history that Tolkien is known for creating.

The story centers on a house cloven by war, an oppressive evil that threatens Humans and Elves, and the adventures, skirmishes, battles, relationships, intrigues, and tragedies that branch out from these dark events. The tale is deftly plotted, gorgeously painted with words, and very emotional.

The scope of **The Children of Húrin** covers several decades, and it has a rich philosophical depth akin to treasured fables, albeit told entirely underneath black clouds in a charcoal grey sky. "For a man that flies from his fear may find that he has only taken a short cut to meet it." Tolkien's book evinces plenty of worldly wisdom.

It wouldn't be wrong to make both Shakespearean and biblical comparisons when discussing Tolkien's prose and dialogue, but the most important things to note are how remote, true, and consistent his writing feels. "A shadow is over you. When we meet again, may it be no darker." Who but Dunsany, Smith, and Howard aimed for and achieved such otherworldly authenticity?

The Children of Húrin ranks very highly on my list of all-time favorite fantasy books, which includes: **Zothique** (Clark Ashton Smith), **The Averoigne Chronicles** (Clark Ashton Smith), **Dreamquest of Unknown Kadath** (H.P. Lovecraft), **Tigana** (Guy Gavriel Kay), **The Lord of the Rings** (J.R.R. Tolkien), **A Song of Ice and Fire** (George R.R. Martin), **Sword of Welleran and Other Stories** (Lord Dunsany), **The Coming of Conan of Cimmeria** (Robert E. Howard), **The Savage Tales of Solomon Kane** (Robert E. Howard), **Magician: Apprentice/Master** (Raymond E. Feist), **The Pastel City** (M. John Harrison), **Throne of Bones** (Brian McNaughton), **Eye of Sounnu** (Schuyler Hernstrom), **Thune's Vision** (Schuyler Hernstrom), **At the Earth's Core** (Edgar Rice Burroughs), **The Sword of Rhiannon** (Leigh Brackett), and **Black Company** (Glen Cook).

Adventurers who seek the glories and sorrows of vanished times and rarely seen places are advised to visit **The Children of Húrin**. This smaller tale is less ambitious than Tolkien's better known works, but it lacks the flaws of those pieces and in some ways is larger in scope and more emotional.

Exhalation by Ted Chiang (2008)
★★★★★

It was amazing.

The finest stories in the second Ted Chiang collection, **Exhalation**, are amongst the most thoughtfully written and thought-provoking works of fiction that I've ever read, and every single piece contained herein is a worthwhile journey. This master craftsman investigates, upends, and inverts big ideas by employing scientific tools: His well considered works are exemplar speculative fiction pieces that touch upon concepts no other genre can explore.

Although I greatly enjoyed Chiang's first collection, **Stories of Your Life and Others**, this new one is richer, more scientifically interesting, and very, very emotionally engaging. (An aside: I didn't care for "Understand" in the first collection — the only story that he's written that I'd describe as commonplace — but I liked or relished all of the others.)

Scientific explorations of religious themes/myths are present in both books, but I prefer "Omphalos" in this new collection over his previous forays ("Hell is the Absence of God," "Seventy-Two Letters," and "Tower of Babylon"), as it cleverly underpins it's religion with science and then makes superb ontological extrapolations from there. The revelations in this piece about the day of creation and cosmology are truly brilliant fictional conceits.

Even though I typically avoid time travel stories, "The Merchant and the Alchemist's Gate" proves that Chiang's talents, humanitarian voice, and clever plotting can create a strong entry in this category. It's a good, somber yet hopeful story.

The ideas explored in the short tales between the long ones are thought-provoking catalysts for discussion on free will ("What's Expected of Us"), communication with non-human beings ("The Great Silence"), and the nature of nurture ("Dacey's Patent Automatic Nanny"). Even these smaller works are valuable jewels.

The two longest tales are amongst the best in the collection. "The Lifecycle of Software Objects" explores Artificial Intelligence in such a way that the treatment of these beings (digients), their development, and the parameters of their worlds mirror our own kindnesses, weaknesses, and biological biases. In this story, Chiang brilliantly reconciles humanity's best traits and flaws with the inexorable, amoral, and valuable advances of science.

"Anxiety is the Dizziness of Freedom" is an exploration that asks questions I've never even considered in relation to divergent quantum realities. As was the case with my favorite story from this author's first collection ("Liking What You See: A Documentary"), thoughtful and believable characters investigate inchoate moral issues that an advancement of science has presented, and the conclusions drawn by the inhabitants of this dizzying web continue to linger in my mind . . .

My other favorite story in the collection, and one of the most daring works in this author's entire catalogue is the titular tale, "Exhalation." This universe is very different from our own: The protagonist's detective work/surgery/scientific musings are odd, memorable, and deftly done, and the thematic connections between this alien place and our own reality only enrich the experience. The bizarre setting of this tale is atypical for Ted Chiang (and feels a bit more like Greg Egan), but Chiang's subtle

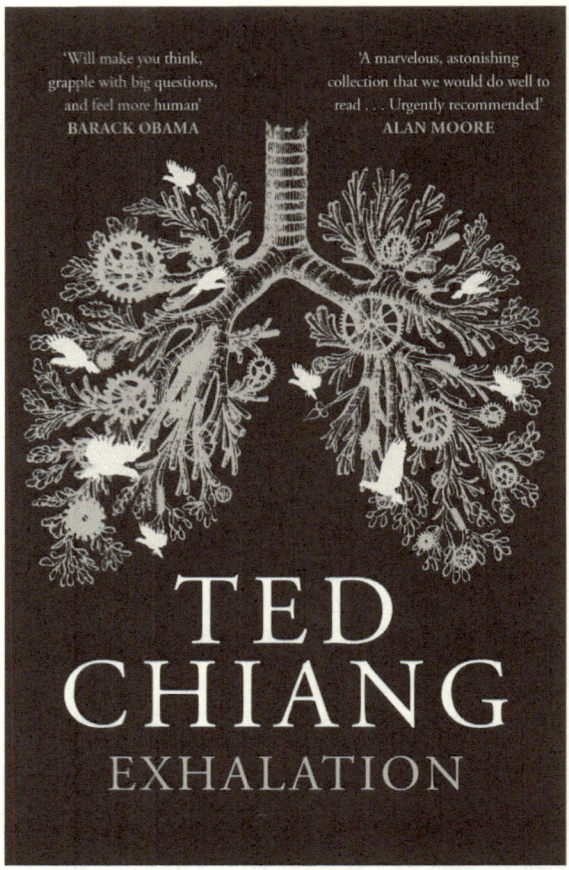

'Will make you think, grapple with big questions, and feel more human'
BARACK OBAMA

'A marvelous, astonishing collection that we would do well to read . . . Urgently recommended'
ALAN MOORE

TED CHIANG
EXHALATION

characterization, warmth, optimism, and introspection are present and make the big, strange ideas resonate universally and feel very personal.

Ted Chiang's second story collection is one of the best science fiction books that I've ever read. I recommend it highly and rank it alongside other favorite works in this genre like **Diaspora** (Greg Egan), **Dark Integers and Other Stories** (Greg Egan), **Quarantine** (Greg Egan), **Appropriate Love** (Greg Egan), **Childhood's End** (Arthur C. Clarke), **Rendezvous with Rama** (Arthur C. Clarke), **Star Maker** (Olaf Stapledon), **Forge of God** (Greg Bear), **The Three Stigmata of Palmer Eldritch** (Philip K. Dick), **Dragon's Egg** (Robert L. Forward), **Left Hand of Darkness** (Ursula K. LeGuin), **The Lotus Eaters** (Stanley G. Weinbaum), **Raft** (Stephen Baxter) and **Black Fog** (Donald Wandrei).

•••

SLEAZE ALLEY

Reviews by Peter Enfantino

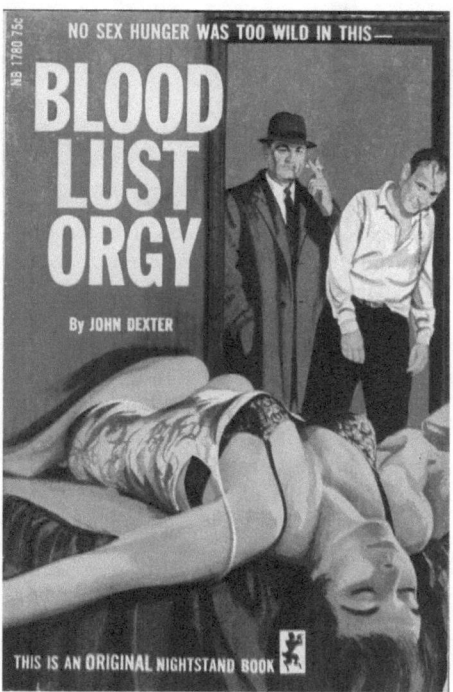

NO SEX HUNGER WAS TOO WILD IN THIS—

BLOOD LUST ORGY

By JOHN DEXTER

THIS IS AN ORIGINAL NIGHTSTAND BOOK

Blood Lust Orgy
by John Dexter (Harry Whittington)
Nightstand Books, March 1966
Cover Artist Unknown
Sex: ★
Story: ★★ 1/2
Cover: ★★ 1/2

The last thing she ever said to him was, "I'll hurry, darling. I'll be right back."

Hooked? I sure was. The story of poor schlepp, Bill Wisdell, and his gorgeous gal, Marge. Their relationship is flourishing, they're both in love, and neither can stand a minute apart. There's only one aspect to this love affair that's a downer: it's an affair. Yep, Marge is married to a loser husband named Gordon who doesn't understand nor appreciate her and it's bringing her down. Bill has nudged Marge to divorce the hubby but back in the 60s, divorce was a little harder to attain, so the intimacy remains in the shadows. Motel rooms and remote lovers' lanes.

After one such tryst in a motel room, Marge insists she has to visit a nearby store to pick up a gift for Gordon so he doesn't suspect she's been doing anything besides window shopping all day. Bill blows a kiss to Marge as she heads into the shop and his life is never the same. An hour later, the worried Bill enters the store and discovers Marge is nowhere in sight. A visit with the owners does nothing to alleviate his frustration and concern but what can a guy do? Could Marge have taken a powder? Maybe she decided this life of illusion won't last and needed to end the affair without a confrontation. Dejected, Bill heads home.

But the worry eats at him and he takes a quick nighttime trip over to Marge's house to see if she's there. Through the front glass, he sees Gordon sitting at his phone, looking just as worried. A car pulls into the driveway and Bill's heart sinks as he sees two detectives climb out of a cop car. Marge is definitely missing.

Knowing that the cops might stumble onto the affair during their investigation, Wisdell visits the police and immediately regrets his honesty when he becomes the main suspect for two bulldog detectives. One of the cops lets on that Marge had once helped the police in a case against a mob bigwig and her testimony had sent the man to jail. Recently released, the mobster has sworn to get even. Could this be the key to cracking the case open?

Well . . . events turn against Bill when Gordon is shot and . . . oh yeah . . . Marge's body is found in Bill's apartment. Now the fuzz are certain they've got the right man so Bill exits stage right, determined to discover the truth behind his true love's grisly slaying.

Blood Lust Orgy starts with a bang and ends with the proverbial whimper. But, oh, that start! If only the entire novel had been as riveting as the first few chapters when we almost *feel* the tension and sympathize with the impossible predicament Bill Wisdell finds himself in. What would anyone do in Bill's situation? Would you keep quiet to avoid scandal and (sure) financial ruin or 'fess up and (hopefully) find your girl safe and in one piece? That turn in the road (about halfway through the novel) is where Harry lost me. From there on, **Blood Lust Orgy** became a standard potboiler with a stultifying reveal. The killer is exactly who we thought he was!

Earl Kemp, editor of Greenleaf, must have thought he had something special here as he waved his "sex scene every ten pages" rule and let Harry be Harry. That aspect of the novel works since, other than an early motel scene between Marge and Bill, only once is the action slowed down for a different kind of action. And that scene, where Bill finds solace and comfort in the arms of a prostitute while searching the streets for Marge, feels awkward and forced. Though I've marveled at several of Whittington's mainstream crime novels (**Web of Murder** and **A Night for Screaming** are both masterpieces of suspense), I've had less success with his sleaze career so far.

A fascinating bit of trivia regarding **Blood Lust Orgy** is that Whittington

A MAD LUST DROVE HIM TO RAVISH AND KILL !

BEAST of SHAME

BY DON HOLLIDAY

A PILLAR BOOK

75¢
PB 847

had sold a novella called "The Crooked Window" to *Shell Scott Mystery Magazine* the year before. Harry added the two flimsy sex scenes, expanded the mob influence, and padded the hell out of "The Crooked Window" and sold it to Kemp as **Blood Lust Orgy**. The condensed version feels rushed after reading the novel but most of the beats are there and it's, at the least, a quicker read.

Beast of Shame
by Don Holliday (David Case)
Pillar, August 1964
Cover Artist Unknown
Sex: ★★★
Story: ★★★ 1/2
Cover: ★★

My first two choices this time around harken back to the early days of the *bare•*bones website when we invited paperback historian Lynn Munroe to choose twenty great "sleaze reads" and two of the picks were **Blood Lust Orgy** and **Beast of Shame**. I've always wanted to read all twenty and I'm slowly but surely making my way through the list (I previously covered **The Lustful Ones** back in issue 1). Both are extremely rare and hard to come by due to their pedigree and subject matter. **Beast of Shame** is David Case's initial foray into horror, a genre he would return to decades later.

There's a werewolf loose in a small town and Detective Joe Bond must sift through the carcasses to come up with some clue as to the beast's real identity. Can Joe track the beast before the next lunar cycle? Early on, we learn the wolf man is actually spoiled rich kid Herod Bryant, whose lycanthropy has evolved from the usual teenage shenanigans: torturing animals and bullying kids at school. Unfortunately, Herod's parents bought their way out of shame and social outcast every time their boy would "act up," and his condition worsened every year. By the time he turned seventeen, if he didn't murder every full moon the boy would undergo severe agony. However, sexual prowess is a plus to the curse and Herod finds himself in bed with lots of sexy women. The downside, of course, is that he feels the need to murder them afterward. Coitus Terminus.

When Bryant's parents are killed in a car crash and he inherits their wealth, all bets are off and the werewolf is free to hit the town whenever that urge arises. Through a series of events, Herod finds himself in love with Joe Bond's wife (who isn't getting the love she needs from her workaholic hubby) but that love doesn't keep him from transforming into a werewolf and thinning out the population of the town. David Case builds the suspense right up to the obligatory showdown between Joe Bond (who's convinced himself he's actually facing a supernatural force) and Herod Bryant.

Though few will rank **Beast of Shame** up there with Leslie Whitten's classic gothic werewolf novel, **Moon of the Wolf**, the novel accomplishes a high level of entertainment. It's fascinating to me that, like **Blood Lust Orgy**, a sex novel like this was published. There's no last second expository cop-out, informing us that Herod simply wore a costume; this guy is an honest-to-goodness werewolf:

The beast snarled again and, crawling,

moved away from its recent prey, leaving the remains sprawled out across the bed. It was gnarled, its face twisted into an impossibly horrible grimace. The lips were pulled far back, baring the fangs.

The final chapter of the novel is reminiscent of Silverberg's **Lust Crew**, an orgy of blood, bones, and violence . . . minus the orgy. **Beast of Shame** never slows down, even in its multitude of sex scenes, and delivers a downbeat climax I never saw coming. Oddly enough, Case never attempts to portray Herod as a sympathetic character nor does he give an explanation for the man's hairy predicament.

In 1980, David Case wrote another werewolf novel, **Wolf Tracks**, published by the fabulously low-budget Belmont Books. That's just been fast-tracked to the top of one of my to-read piles.

Lust Lover
by Dan Eliot (Robert Silverberg)
Pillar, September 1963
Cover Artist Unknown
Sex: ★★
Story: ★★★ 1/2
Cover: ★★★

Lou Andreas can't understand why his hobby isn't more popular; Lou is a serial killer. Rocketing out of a bad encounter with an ill-mannered prostitute, teenage Lou begins murdering hookers and getting very good at hiding any traces of the culprit. So good in fact, the authorities don't seem to detect any patterns in Lou's schedule. Of course, the fact that his victims are working girls might have something to do with that.

Wanting to maintain a life outside of homicide, Lou takes up with a girl named Tony, who's both gorgeous and intelligent. After a few months of canoodling and soft-core sex, Tony wants Lou to marry her and to attain that goal she allows herself to become pregnant. No woman will tie Lou down, however, and he quickly finds a way to weasel out of a shotgun wedding. He joins the army and is shipped out to Germany and he and Tony never see each other again. While Lou was bedding Tony,

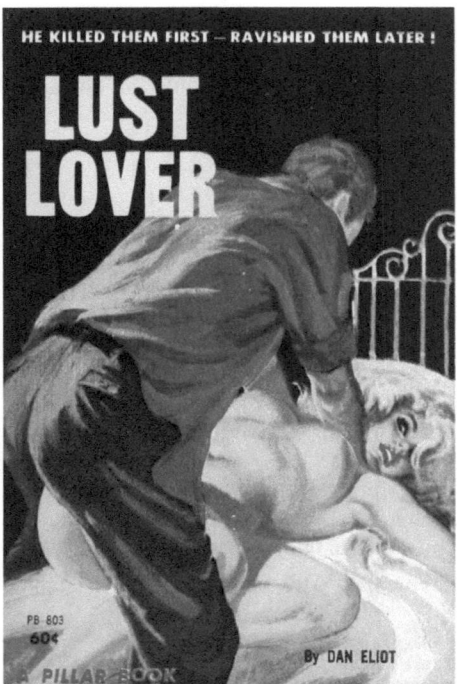

HE KILLED THEM FIRST — RAVISHED THEM LATER !

LUST LOVER

PB-803
60¢

By DAN ELIOT

A PILLAR BOOK

his extracurricular activities tailed off but now, with lots of time and plenty of foreign women to choose from, Lou turns it up several notches.

Exiting the service, Andreas becomes a traveling salesman, a perfect compliment to his "career of assassination."

The bulk of the book is given over to a retelling of Lou Andreas's teen years and his unique "hobby." Lou stumbles into his first kill by accident but then finds the act so thrilling that it must be repeated. Silverberg's account of the first murder is unnerving:

It was a moment he never forgot. There was the sudden delicious shock wave that came rippling up his arm as the first heavy blow crashed into her head, and there was the immediate thud of her body hitting the floor. The bottle did not break. But her skull did. A little surprised at the strength he had put into the blow, Andreas stared down at her and saw the blood come seeping out into her hair, matting it and staining it bright red.

He knelt.

He lifted the bottle again.

He had to be certain she was really dead.

He brought the bottle down, clublike, a

second time, a third, a fourth. He hit her again and again, until her head was only so much soggy pulp. It had split like an eggshell, and fragments of brain oozed out. He took care not to let any of it get on his clothing.

After this murder, Andreas keeps it simple, strangling his victims (these scenes may be less graphic but they're no less disconcerting) and then performing sexual acts on the bodies, post mortem. A trip back to home town Cleveland turns out to be the killer's undoing when he spies the prostitute who mocked him a decade before and decides to pay her back. Unfortunately for Lou, the woman has seen the error of her ways and become a vice cop. Turns out the police have been setting a net up for Lou ever since his previous strangling.

Lust Lover is the fourth Greenleaf by Robert Silverberg I've read and the best since **Lust Crew**, both similar in their staggering bursts of violence. Through all the gruesomeness, Silverberg maintains a sense of humor, as in when Andreas decides to "play a game" with himself and murder a woman in each town that has a major league baseball team (*The National League took a little longer.*). The author may have been pumping out one of these a month (and stocking the sleaze crime digests and sci-fi mags regularly as well) but you'd never know from the level of professionalism displayed. Lou Andreas is a compelling, complicated creature, not just a simple mama's boy reverting to primitive urges due to a slight. There are several junctures in the novel where you feel you know which path Silverberg is leading you, only to have the rug pulled out. That's my favorite kind of read.

Obsession with Lust
by S. V. Baxter
Candid Reader, November 1969
Cover Artist Unknown
Sex: ★★★ 1/2
Story: ★★★
Cover: ★★★

Being the life and amorous adventures of well-endowed lotharia Shane Baxter, from his days seducing his college teacher to working London streets to his stint with Madame Corrienne and her *Le Pucce Fosse* (The Flea Pit) sex theater in Paris. Can wandering spirit Shane find love in a world dependent upon multiple orgasms?

Obsession with Lust defies the usual synopsis in that a plot description would be maddeningly incoherent (as mine above clearly shows) since the novel is made up of spurts and forks in the road, with the spurts being literal as well. Shane has a best friend / roommate / circle jerk buddy named Warren who is an integral part of the first third of the book but then is unceremoniously discarded and hardly mentioned the rest of the way. Shane's stint with a pimp in London is similarly brief and jettisoned as is his dalliance with the Flea Pit. It's as though author S. V. Baxter became bored with the way things were progressing and decided to change gears four times and couldn't be bothered to restructure what he'd already committed to manuscript.

All this might have doomed another novel but I found the frequent layovers and plane changes in **Obsession** to be refreshingly "true to life," and every new stop was intriguing. Where Shane eventually lands seems, in the same way, to be organic but might put some readers off. Even though the prose is literate, author Baxter clearly remembers what he was hired for. Since **Obsession** was published in the no-holds-barred era of Greenleaf, Baxter maintains an approximate pace of two paragraphs human interest, two pages hardcore sex. We have no idea who Baxter really was (the only other Greenleaf Baxter is credited with is **Sex Maniac**), but the guy could string together some very readable sentences in between the coupling:

She drove like a maniac, without the slightest display of nerves. Our destination was the Albert Hall, where a celebrated but freakish type of entertainer recently arrived from the States was giving one of his bizarre performances. The act was popular among the swinging set. I found it nauseating but tolerably compensating, but my thoughts were preoccupied with sex. Lucy had made a tremendous impact on my physical senses.

Baxter's sex scenes alternate between stock cliche and erotic, depending upon Shane's surroundings, but also go into realms I'd not encountered in a Greenleaf before (and would rather avoid in the future!), such as "golden showers" and bestiality. Fortunately, those lapses are few and most of the screwing is done with "hardcore good taste" (if there is such a thing):

I thrust my hand between her thighs before she could stop me, felt her whole body tense and stiffen, her legs come together. Slowly, she relaxed, allowed me to fondle the soft lips of her quim, then pushed me away abruptly.

"That's it, for now," she said. "Now put that gorgeous thing away before you come all over the carpet and spoil everything."

The Candid Reader line began in 1967 and published 148 titles until the imprint was abandoned in 1970. Because prolific artist Robert Bonfils painted nearly sixty of the covers that graced the Candids, the line is immensely popular with collectors and can fetch obscene prices online.

TO CATCH A SINNER HE HAD TO BECOME ONE!

LUST TYCOON

75c

BY
J. X. WILLIAMS

NB 1727

THIS IS A *NEW* NIGHTSTAND BOOK

Lust Tycoon
by J. X. Williams
Nightstand Books, February 1965
Cover Artist Unknown
Sex: ★
Story: ★★ 1/2
Cover: ★★

Disgraced cop Tom Dash quits the force and buys a ketch (a large sailboat); he sinks thousands into renovating the boat (nicknamed *Sitting Pretty*) and then opens a touristy sightseeing business. This is how Tom meets Bridgett Beauregard, a pretty young thing who happens to be fluent in "plotting and navigation," and the two hit it off immediately. Dash hires the girl as a sort of first mate and, naturally, intimacy follows very quickly. Bridgett, however, comes with enormous baggage. She was once married to an abusive multimillionaire and still cringes at the mention of the man.

The two sail out one day in inclement weather and Bridgett mysteriously disappears from the boat while Dash has his attention on getting them back to land safely. Though he looks everywhere, Bridgett is not to be found. Tom calls the cops and suspicion is immediately cast on the ex-cop; the local detectives know all about Dash's sketchy career and how he left the job. They're not likely to be sympathetic to his plight. The third degree only gets more intense when Bridgett's body washes ashore, a bullet hole scarring what's left of her shark-gnawed corpse.

Dash concludes that if Bridgett's killer is to be apprehended, he'll have to use his own knowledge of detection and deception to get the job done. Following up on a solid lead, Dash overhears a man and woman plotting a murder; oddly enough, the man turns out to be Richard Troy, an ex-con Dash sent up years before. When the amateur PI's cover is blown, Troy comes after him with a gun and Dash is forced to clobber the guy with a chair. Later, while listening to a news report, Dash discovers both Troy and his girl were murdered after he fled and Dash is the number one suspect. Now the hunter is the hunted.

I know what you're saying right now: Um, excuse me, Mr. Alley, where's the sleaze? Well, that's a good question. Other than a brief tryst in a country cabin while on the run, Tom Dash keeps his pants on for the duration of **Lust Tycoon**. This is, in fact, the least sleaziest sleaze novel I've ever read. But that's not the problem with the book. After a wholly involving introduction and first half that continued to draw me in, the second half became nothing but a standard (albeit well-written) mystery thriller, which leads to a ludicrous climax.

Perhaps the action should have remained revolved around the harbor and the *Sitting Pretty* (as was the case with Jeff Tyler and his yacht, the *Loafalong* in **Jambalaya Loverman**, reviewed back in *bare•bones* 5) since, once Dash takes to the city, the novel becomes just another "Wrong Man" riff. That being said, **Lust Tycoon** is a decent enough thriller that, with a few tweaks, might have hit the paperback stands with a Dell or Avon banner across its cover.

•••

I stood on King Kong's actual head and lived to tell the tale.

No, really.

The knee-slapper part is that it took me a quarter of a century to figure it out.

The deduction part was polluted by too many of what important scientists call "KS Variables," "KS" standing for "kinda-sorta." It wasn't *the* King Kong, yet almost certainly *a* King Kong . . . kinda-sorta. One of many. Because sequels, remakes, stunt parts, stand-ins, doubles and triples, replacements, fakes. Among a plethora of subsequent King Kongs — which one might this be, if any?

Researchers who know this eggshell dilemma will be wincing already.

For example, the "actual" claim in the opening line above is conditional, since movie history has known more than a few "actual" Kongs. Upfront: No, I'm not talking about the original, classic, immortal Kong from 1933. That one — if we take as gospel the assertion of Eli Cross in *The Stunt Man* — was only *"three foot six!"* So I missed severely damaging the Eighth Wonder of the World by striking a pose atop his tiny model head.

In order to validate this recollect I must presume that you already know the name Dino DeLaurentiis.

About thirty years ago, I plus a group of like-minded individuals were busy working on a little film titled *The Crow* at what was then called Carolco Studios in Wilmington, North Carolina. If you ask the people who hang around the Cape Fear Museum (yes, we were hawking distance from the really-truly Cape Fear), they'll tell you that "Wilmy-wood" was born in 1983 when Frank Capra Jr. was scouting locations for *Firestarter*. His cohort, Dino D., saw the opportunity to establish a full-blown studio facility far from the maggot madness of Hollywood Improper, and DEG Studios was born. (Short for "De Laurentiis Entertainment Group." I still have a desk lamp with a "Property of DEG" logo sticker on it.)

DEG literally revitalized the dying town of Wilmington. It created jobs and attracted

Photo: John Bergin

the industry to support those jobs, becoming a hub for both feature film and TV production. It had soundstages and an actual paved backlot. Even better, it was situated in a right-to-work state that offered financial incentives and tax credits to attract production. This hot period sputtered out by 2014, by which time the new showbiz mecca had become Atlanta, Georgia.

We got there after DEG had gone bankrupt and the facility had become the even-more-notorious Carolco Studios. We poached a standing set for *Matlock* as our police station. The Coen Brothers were shooting *The Hudsucker Proxy* on whatever stages we weren't using … which is how I got to meet Paul Newman, for the only time in my life.

Beyond the soundstages was the backlot that became Wrench Street for *The Crow*. It was our entire exterior city as you see it in the film, apart from model, process, and soundstage portions. (For a comparison view of the same set, take a look at the muddy city street in *The Road to Wellville*.) And behind the building false fronts (which went up about three stories), 75 feet from the rear property line, there was a vast junkyard of discarded "movie

stuff," including the fiberglass front of the Green Goblin truck from *Maximum Overdive* (1986). which had been sitting back there getting overgrown by weeds for seven years.

There were discarded building shells burned by pyro. Junk columns and lumber from obsolete sets, left to rot in the weather. Paint cans, trash, all manner of detritus — a general dumping ground. Locals called it the Boneyard.

There were King Kong parts back there in the high grass.

I assumed the parts were from the lamentable *King Kong Lives* (1986), because there was a kind of "show head" parked out in front of the model shop. (I heard this auxiliary Kong head later wound up near the studio front gate. If anyone knows its ultimate fate, ping us!)

Crow storyboard artist Peter Pound and I shot a lot of video and took many still photos during our more than one hundred days on set. We'd hand cameras off to each other on the fly. We wandered the wreckage of the *Crow* cemetery the day after the '93 Superstorm blew it away. (Our tombstones were styrofoam, so you can imagine the carnage.) As we poked about the Boneyard, and Peter snapped the photo below.

Please note that this is ***not*** the same head as the Aux Head pictured to the right. In fact, it's barely recognizable as a head at all. It's pointed upward and I'm sitting on the jaw. You can see the brow on the right side of the photo. I was basically looking right at two large plasticine-coated eyes which were impossible to budge (or remove) since they were rusted into some very complicated, rock-solid mounts of machined aluminum with zero wiggle room.

Not the head I mean. Peter Pound with video camera.

It slowly occurred to Peter and I that the wreckage strewn all over the back of the backlot was ***far too complex and intricate*** to be fallout from *King Kong Lives*, which had a purported all-in budget of $10 million. We found incredibly articulated giant hands of stainless steel festooned with pistons and decaying rubber hoses. Everything was bolted, welded, and custom-built . . . *over*-built, in fact. Every single aspect of every single finger of that hand had been made-to-order from scratch.

The hands looked exactly like this:

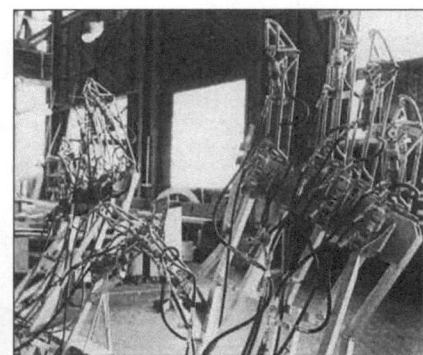

Given Carlo Rambaldi's infamously overcomplicated, time-sucking "engineering" that hardly ever worked properly across multiple movie assignments, the stuff surrounding us like a disassembled behemoth skeleton could easily have cost from

DJS on Kong head in the Boneyard.

two to three million to fabricate — in short, the ballpark price quote for Rambaldi's so-called "robot" Kong. In 1980, **Kong '76** screenwriter Lorenzo Semple Jr. told **Starlog**:

> "That was Dino's grandiose dream — millions of dollars were wasted in constructing a 40-foot tall mechanical ape that was technically impossible to execute."

Or put another way: six and a half tons of stainless steel, aluminum, horsehair, plastic, rubber and hydraulics that could barely spasm on command without locking up or blowing a hose.

And it *still* hadn't dawned on me that perhaps I was perched on top of Carlo's masterwork. Because I'd heard numerous stories about that mega-Kong being junked, along with the $300,000 foam Kong corpse used for the crowd shots after KK's big fall from World Trade. Supposedly that Kong had been ripped to shreds by souvenir hunters following its glory shot for the end of the '76 movie.

No it wasn't, because it showed up in Buenos Aires in 1978 (below). Maybe the Argentinians shredded it. *Maybe delinquent birds pecked it to death.*

You'll find Not-So-Mecha-Kong's 1978 adventure in South America covered in detail by a 2017 post online at *Corroded Vault*. Shipped in eighteen gigantic crates moved by several flatbed trucks, it was erected on a sort of stone grotto set where it would twitch and roar and (it is said) even answer audience questions. (Part of the audience spiel posited that Kong was "the enemy of Superman," since the 1978 Richard Donner movie was about to premiere.) Merch and photo ops aplenty. Clowns and jugglers. More or less the carnival atmosphere Dino had tried to evoke in the Big Apple.

The roughly 20-minute show went on for four months, and then moved to the beach city Mar de Plata, where they had to dig a pit to house it and a circus tent to cover it (opposite). As locals said, they had to "build a moat in order to build an amphitheater."

If you want a really deep dive into all this, an obsessive fellow named Fernando Jorge Soto Roland wrote an entire monograph titled "Kong's Tooth" in 2015. His work is thorough, but unfortunately invests far too much time on conspiracy-theory-flavored sideroads of inquiry into military dictatorships, the history of free-market capitalism, and the odd claim that there

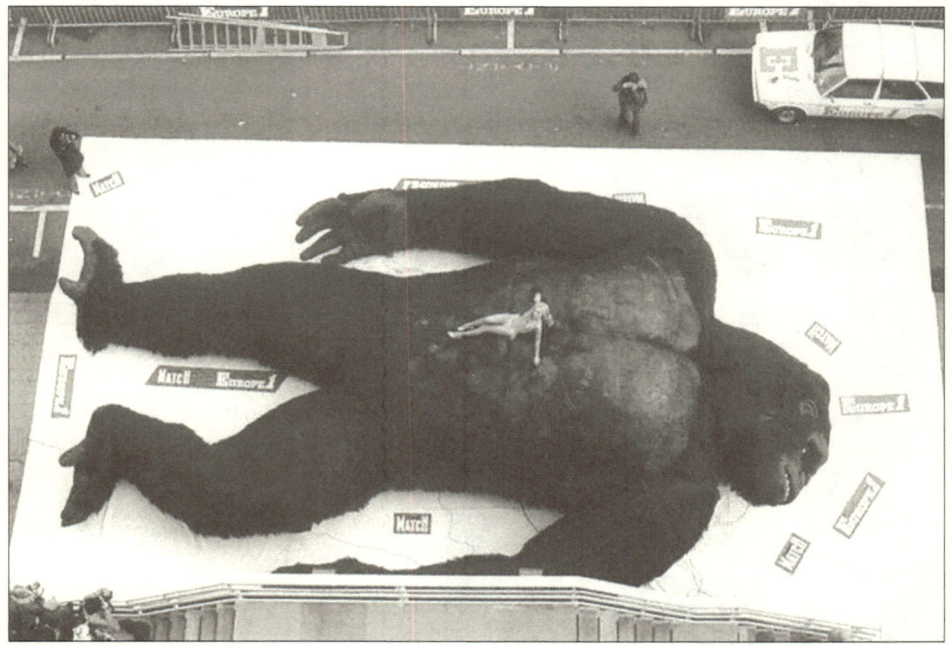

the monkey from Dino D's Academy Award-winning cinematic extravaganza. See the film *Ciao Maschio* (aka *Bye Bye, Monkey*, 1978), about a baby chimpanzee adopted as Kong's orphaned son by Gérard Depardieu and Marcello Mastroianni after they discover the "discarded" 1976 movie Kong in a Hudson River landfill.

(Spoiler: They do *not* discover the discarded 1976 movie Kong, but another immobile "doll" not nearly as big.)

At this point my brain began to swim with the possibility I was bending facts to fit my preferred thesis. That Kong was, in fact, standing on *my* head rather than the other way around in a classic case of confirmation bias.

But what of Rambaldi's genuine "cybernetic masterwork," so-called by the usual press puffery run rampant?

More South American misadventures ensued, until the *Wilmington Morning Star* reported, in an article by Gina White (27 April 1985): "Hollywood's Most Famous Ape Arrives at his Final Resting Place":

were actually *two* full-sized, mechanical Kongs, one of which supposedly burned up at Universal Studios Florida long after the incursion of the Carlo Kong noted here.

Fans of *Contact* will understand the notion.

Granted, another Kong *had* been built for ballyhoo in Sao Paulo back in 1977, but it was just a statue and significantly shorter than the bona fide Rambaldi clockwork wonderment. It appeared for 90 days at an amusement park called Playcenter and then was shuffled around the country.

What became of that one? Some mysteries are doomed to irresolution.

At least Fernando's investigation explains why there were no teeth in the Kong head I stumbled across on the backlot. They had been purloined while Kong was tucked under a tarp at a trucking company warehouse before being shipped to Brazil for further exploitation. Between whistle-stops, Kong would get new dentures. Which would then be stolen at the next port of call. And so on.

The "two dolls" theory belies a chronic misunderstanding of how Hollywood finances usually work. Ordinary citizens generally assume a money faucet that never cranks off, overlooking the codicil that most motion picture big-bucks exist to be stolen or skimmed, not deployed. No way would Dino squander additional mega-millions to clone a catastrophe that didn't work in the first place, especially when there was no chance of a sequel, Oscars be damned.

There was, yes, of course, *another* puppet fated to be hawked to a gullible public as

> . . . all 20 tons of him . . . tattered and torn but generally intact, the 57-foot creature arrived Tuesday — and Wednesday — after a nine-day journey from MGM's Los Angeles Studios . . . "It went on a road show around the world," said Eddie Surkin, a special effects creator who built and engineered the creature . . . Argentina, Brazil and Europe are among the places the mechanical monkey has visited. He also appeared at amusement parks and the circus . . . because of his heavy weight, special routes and only 250 miles of travel were permitted each day . . .

You'll find Eddie Surkin credited as "mechanical coordinator" on the '76 movie. A 2017 interview with him (not about *Kong*) is still available online.

I think the thing that really cinched it for

me was this photo right here, posted on the "Port of Long Beach" Twitter page in 2013.

The Crow came to Carolco Studios right after *Super Mario Brothers* had shot in Wilmington. As soon as we wrapped, *The Hudsucker Proxy* performed overnight urban renewal on the former Wrench Street and dusted it in artificial snow for a single shot. (They could do that sort of thing because they had ten million bucks more in their budget than we did.)

But a negligence lawsuit brought against Carolco by one of our carpenters, Jim Martishius, prompted a code-red scramble to clean up the Boneyard, where Jim had been horribly injured on our first day of filming. The lawsuit involved the constantly-morphing placement of power poles and electric lines to service the continuously-shifting needs of different set configurations. Too easy, it was, to run afoul of a live wire that wasn't there yesterday, or wasn't live yesterday. Carolco had run the required inspections and pronounced the area safe. It wasn't. Jim was blinded in his right eye and burned over 45% of his body. I remember attending a benefit for him a couple of nights later, an event organized by his friends and co-workers. No producers were present.

In 1999, Jim eventually won a huge trial-by-jury judgement against Carolco. Another two years were eaten by appeals and such, but Jim prevailed. (He was still working as a prop and construction foreman as of 2019.)

By contrast, the Boneyard ceased to exist in record time. It was gone even before we finished shooting *The Crow*.

Then the entire backlot — every bolt and splinter of Wrench Street — got erased as well. Eliminated. Bulldozed. Backlots tend not to age well. Rickety fake buildings intended to last for two weeks of shooting stay creaking in the breeze and are re-used for years. Wood rots. Insulation crumbles. Supports warp and fail. And most of the depreciation is invisible until it falls apart or catches fire.

Cutthroat Island prompted Carolco's bankruptcy in 1995, and the whole shebang became EUE/Screen Gems Ltd. The entire 43-acre lot was renovated and expanded. Stage 10 now sits where our backlot used to be.

Along with the Boneyard, Kong had vanished mysteriously once again. But I'm satisfied that I actually sat atop "Rambaldi's Folly" for real. I had witnesses.

Fight me!

•••

KONGALLERY!

As a bonus tie-in to DJS' Kong coverage, *bare•bones* is pleased to bring you the following selection of mechanical Kong shots! — John

A GOOD CAST IS WORTH REPEATING

Matthew R. Bradley is the author of **Richard Matheson on Screen: A History of the Filmed Works** (McFarland, 2010) and the co-editor, with Stanley Wiater and Paul Stuve, of **The Richard Matheson Companion** (Gauntlet, 2008). He is preparing a comprehensive screen history of the "California Sorcerers" writers' group that included Robert Bloch, Ray Bradbury, George Clayton Johnson, Matheson, William F. Nolan, Jerry Sohl (all of whom he interviewed extensively), and Charles Beaumont. He also explores "the nexus of film and literature" at his blog, Bradley on Film (https://bradleyonfilm.wordpress.com).

J. Charles Burwell is a long-time reader and collector of vintage paperbacks and pulps. For over forty years, he has been both an aficionado and admittedly amateur scholar of Hardboiled, Noir, and Western fiction. Beginning with a tattered Dell Mapback edition of Dashiell Hammett's **Nightmare Town,** his collection expanded to include copies of *Black Mask, Manhunt,* and paperback originals published by Gold Medal and Lion. He also collects the paperback covers of Avati, Meltzoff, and Zuckerberg. Author of an as-yet unpublished hitch-hiking memoir, **Going East, Will Share Gas**, he is currently at work on a collection, **Strange Tales of the '70s.** He can be reached at zenoir@optonline.net

Gilbert Colon is a contributor-at-large for *bare•bones* e-zine and *Marvel University.* His work has also appeared in *Cinema Retro, Filmfax, Strand Mystery Magazine, CSL: The Bulletin of the New York C.S. Lewis Society,* SF Signal, the St. Martin's Press newsletter Tor.com, and several other outlets. His interview with filmmaker Abel Ferrara (**New Rose Hotel**) appeared in the Stark House Press book *Invasion of the Body Snatchers: A Tribute.* He can be reached at gcolon777@gmail.com

Peter Enfantino is the co-author of **The Manhunt Companion** (Stark House, 2021) and an obsessive collector of Mystery, Crime and Horror digests including *Alfred Hitchcock, Manhunt, Mike Shayne,* as well as the entire stable of Warren Magazines. He has written for all the major channels on the topics, including *Paperback Parade, Mystery Scene, The Digest Enthusiast, Paperback Fanatic, Monster Maniac, Men of Violence, Mystery File, Comic Effect,* and Peter Normanton's *From the Tomb.* He is currently working on an exhaustive critical guide to the Atlas Pre-Code Horror Comic Books. In his spare time, he writes with Jack Seabrook on DC War comics, the Warren Publishing phenomenon, and Batman in the 1980s. He Lives in Gilbert, Arizona.

Richard Krauss is the editor and publisher of *The Digest Enthusiast,* a book/magazine that explores the world of digest magazines through interviews, articles, and reviews. It also includes original genre fiction. Krauss is also the designer for Alec Cizak's *Pulp Modern* and several standalone volumes such as Roman Scott's **Oddities and Other Grotesques,** Clark Dissmeyer's **Through a Basement Window** (both edited by Marc Myers), and Bruce Chrislip's **The Minicomix Revolution 1969–1989.** (larquepress.com)

William Schoell is the author of eleven novels and twenty-one non-fiction books including **The Horror Comics: Fiends, Freaks and Fantastic Creatures** and **Creature Features: Nature Turned Nasty in the Movies.** His horror novels include **Saurian, Vicious,** and **Things That Go Bump in the Night;** all are available from Cemetery Dance publishers as e-books. His movie blogs are *Great Old Movies* (greatoldmovies.blogspot.com) and *B Movie Nightmare* (bmovienightmare.blogspot.com).

David J. Schow is a multiple-award-winning West Coast writer. The latest of his ten novels is a hardboiled extravaganza called **The Big Crush** (2019). The newest of his eleven short story collections is a compendium titled **Monster Movies** (2020). He has been a contributor to Storm King Comics' **John Carpenter's Tales for a Halloween Night** since its very first issue. In 2021, Storm King released his eight-issue series **John Carpenter's Tales of Science Fiction** — "Hell," now available in a collected trade paperback. DJS has written extensively for film (*The Crow, Leatherface: Texas Chainsaw Massacre III, The Hills Run Red*) and television (*Masters of Horror, Mob City, Creepshow*). His nonfiction works include **The Art of Drew Struzan** (2010) and **The Outer Limits at 50** (2014). He can be seen on various DVDs as expert witness or documentarian on everything from *Creature from the Black Lagoon* to *Psycho* to *I, Robot*, not to mention the Rondo and Saturn Award-winning *Outer Limits* (Seasons 1 and 2) discs from Kino-Lorber and Via Vision. Thanks to him, the word "splatterpunk" has been in the Oxford English Dictionary since 2002.

John Scoleri is the author of several books on artist Ralph McQuarrie, including **The Art of Ralph McQuarrie: ARCHIVES** (Dreams & Visions Press, 2015), and the producer of the DVDs *Ralph McQuarrie: Illustrator* (2002) and *Caroline Munro: First Lady of Fantasy* (2004). Publications under his Cimarron Street Books imprint include the works of David J. Schow, Robert Colby's **The Devil's Collector**, the magazine you're currently holding and the forthcoming **Raiders of the Lost Art: The Unseen Designs of Movie Tie-In Solicitation Covers**. He curates the **I Am Legend** Archive (iamlegendarchive. com) from his home in Santa Clara, California, where he continues to work on **Latent Images** (Dreams & Visions Press), a photographic retrospective of George A. Romero's *Night of the Living Dead*.

Jay Shepard has been a reader of *Star Wars* fiction since 1978, and was the host of *Jedi Journals* — a monthly *Star Wars* literature podcast — from 2011 to 2021. He was also a writer and editor on the *Star Wars* fansite rebelscum.com, and was responsible for maintaining its online database of *Star Wars* literature; also called *Jedi Journals*. Currently, he hosts *Superhero Suite*, a podcast about all-things superhero related, writes weekly *Sci-Fi Saturdays* articles for RetroZap.com, and maintains a list of filming locations for the Marvel Cinematic Universe at MCULocationScout.com.

S. Craig Zahler is an award-winning screenwriter, director, novelist, cinematographer, and musician. He wrote, directed, and co-composed the score for the 2015 film *Bone Tomahawk*, an Independent Spirit Award nominated picture (Best Screenplay; Best Supporting Actor) starring Kurt Russell. Zahler also wrote and directed *Brawl in Cell Block 99*, a *New York Times* Critic's Pick, starring Vince Vaughn. Both movies were added to the permanent collection of the Museum of Modern Art in New York City in 2017. Mel Gibson and Vince Vaughn star in Zahler's new crime drama *Dragged Across Concrete*. Zahler's debut western novel, **A Congregation of Jackals** was nominated for the Peacemaker and the Spur awards, and his 2014 novels **Mean Business on North Ganson Street** and **Corpus Chrome, Inc.** both received starred reviews for excellence in *Booklist*. His book **Hug Chickenpenny: The Panegyric of an Anomalous Child** is a gothic tale will bring to the silver screen with the help of his new creative partners, The Jim Henson Company. After reading this strange story, Clive Baker declared, "S. Craig Zahler is certain to become one of the great imaginers of our time." His latest novel is **The Slanted Gutter**.

back·issues

TSF #1 - SOLD OUT

TSF #2 - SOLD OUT

TSF #3 - $15

TSF #7 - $15

TSF #8 - SOLD OUT

TSF #9 - SOLD OUT

TSF #13 - SOLD OUT

TSF #14 - $15

TSF #15 - SOLD OUT

TSF #19 - $20

NOTLD - SOLD OUT

BB #1 - $15

Supplies are limited. Prices do not include shipping.

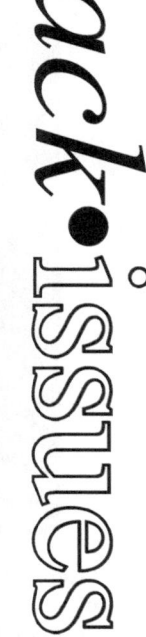

back•issues

TSF #4 - SOLD OUT

TSF #5 - $7

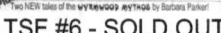

TSF #6 - SOLD OUT

TSF #10 - $15

TSF #11 - $15

TSF #12 - $25

TSF #16 - $20

TSF #17 - $15

TSF #18 - $15

BB #2 - $10
(2020 Reprint)

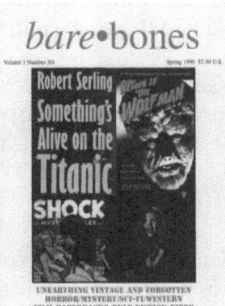

BB #3/4 - $10
Magazine-Sized
Double Issue

BB #5 - $10
(2020 Reprint)

BB #6 - $10

For ordering information, contact: CimarronStreetBooks@gmail.com

It's not too late to catch up on the best of *The Scream Factory* (1988-1997) or the original *bare•bones* (1997-2001)

From 1988-1997, *The Scream Factory* provided an exhaustive and often irreverent overview of all aspects of horror—from fiction to film and beyond. It became a go-to reference for horror aficionados around the globe. 20 years after the magazine ceased publication, the editors have sifted through the contents of the magazine's 20-issue run to assemble this 590-page 8.5" x 11" epic collection.

The Best of The Scream Factory ($29.95 TPB) reprints more than 70 articles from the magazine's golden age, covering such diverse topics as: the best horror novels of the '80s; a viewer's guide to Godzilla movies; horror in the pulps; the worst in horror; dark suspense fiction; the influence of *Night of the Living Dead* on fiction and film; horror on old-time radio; sci-fi/horror hybrids; western horror; werewolf fiction; British horror fiction and films; Canadian horrors; and horror in the comics. In addition to the nearly 600-page selection of "greatest hits," the editors have penned a brand new 25,000 word introduction!

Born from the ashes of *The Scream Factory*, *bare•bones* (1997-2001) unearthed some of the best vintage and forgotten paperbacks, films, pulp fiction, television, and video. *bare•bones — the best of —* ($16.95 TPB/$22.95 HC) collects many of the best articles from the magazine's original run, including:

- Overviews of fiction series including: George Chesbro's Mongo, Robert Lory's Dracula, Richard Stark's Parker, John Sanford's Prey novels, Karl Edward Wagner's Kane, and the Black novels of Cornell Woolrich!
- Retrospectives on filmmakers Edward L. Cahn and Jerry Warren!
- An overview of the Blind Dead films!
- Ann-Margret movie tie-ins!
- Annotated Indexes to *Saturn Science Fiction* and *Web Detective Stories*!
- A detailed overview of the *Dark Shadows* novels of Dan (Marilyn) Ross!
- Commentary on Trevanian and Top Ten lists by David J. Schow!
- A look back at the *Trilogy of Terror* Zuni!
- Interviews with Bill Crider, Richard Prather, Robert Serling and Bay Area *Creature Features* horror host Bob Wilkins!

Order today on Amazon, eBay or through CimarronStreetBooks@gmail.com!

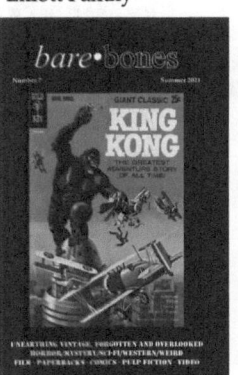

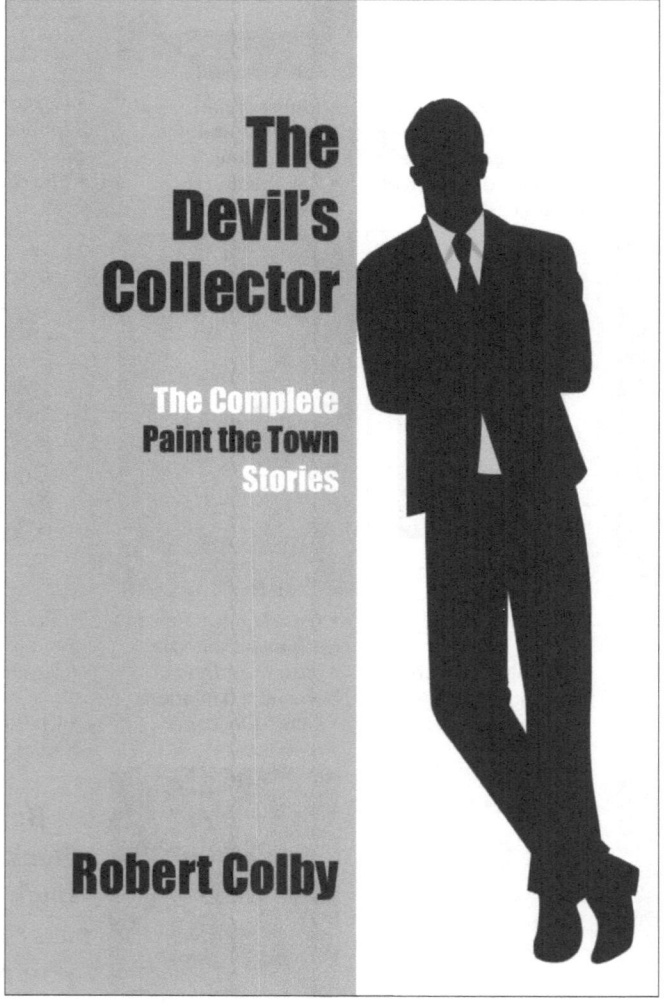

Havoc Swims Jaded musters another lucky 13 short stories by *David J. Schow*, who has won awards for this sort of behavior.

Havoc reigns as a bullet-filled criminal named Leadman goes totally aggro, and a prehistoric, Lagoony creature engages in mortal combat with his own evolved self.

Havoc ensues, as a time-displaced trio of friends find themselves lost in a trackless desert zone where there are no "signposts up ahead" at twilight. As your friendly TV remote control displays disturbing new functions. As changing your body image becomes as simple as donning a zip-up human suit.

Havoc cries forth the ghosts of the dogs of war as the Berlin Wall falls, in the novella-length "Dismantling Fortress Architecture."

These and other dark tales of disturbance await the pleasure of your discomfiture. You will find, as Peter Straub said, that "here, all of Schow's glittering weapons are sharper than ever before."

Cimarron Street Books is pleased to bring you World Fantasy Award-winning author **David J. Schow**'s seventh short story collection, for the first time in paperback, featuring an updated afterword, an extensive essay on all-things Creature from the Black Lagoon, and fully illustrated with the artwork of Woody Welch and Bernie Wrightson.

Caroline Munro
FIRST LADY OF FANTASY

Made in United States
Troutdale, OR
12/27/2023

16499691R00072